ABSTRACT EXPRESSIONS

A
COLORING
BOOK

BY VALERIE DOWDY

Dedication
Ashley Shaun & Cassandra
For always believing I can do anything
Love you most,
Mom

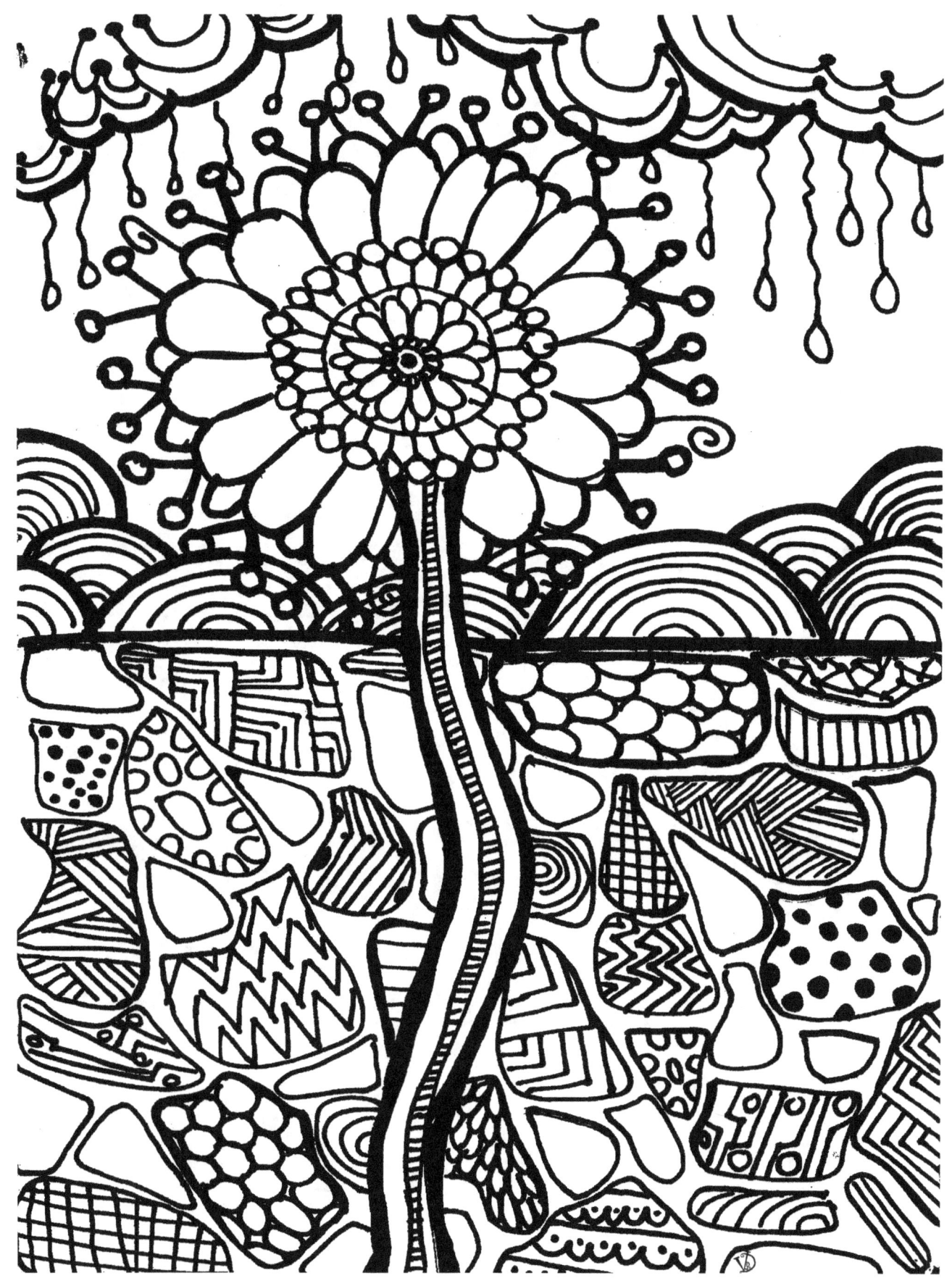

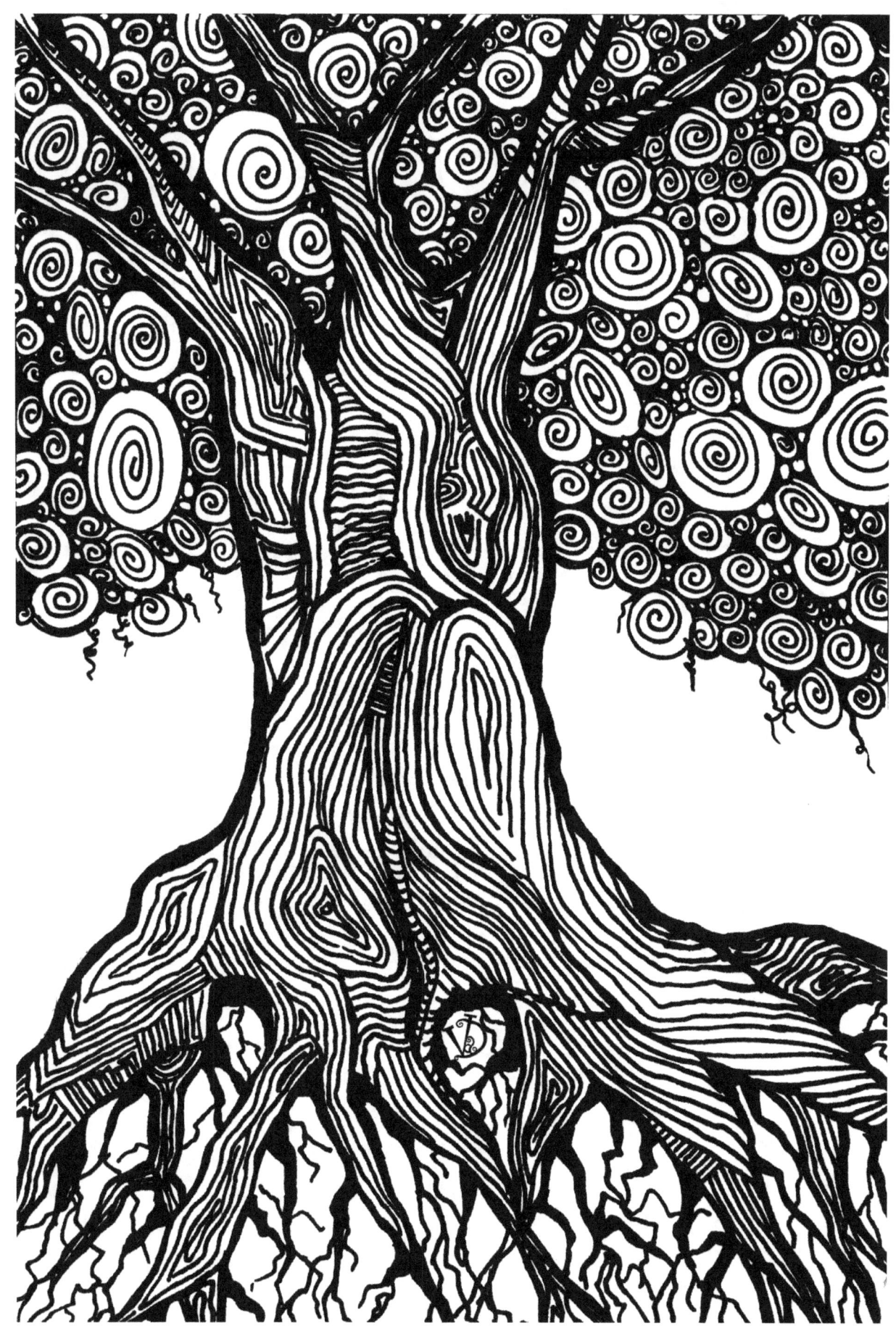

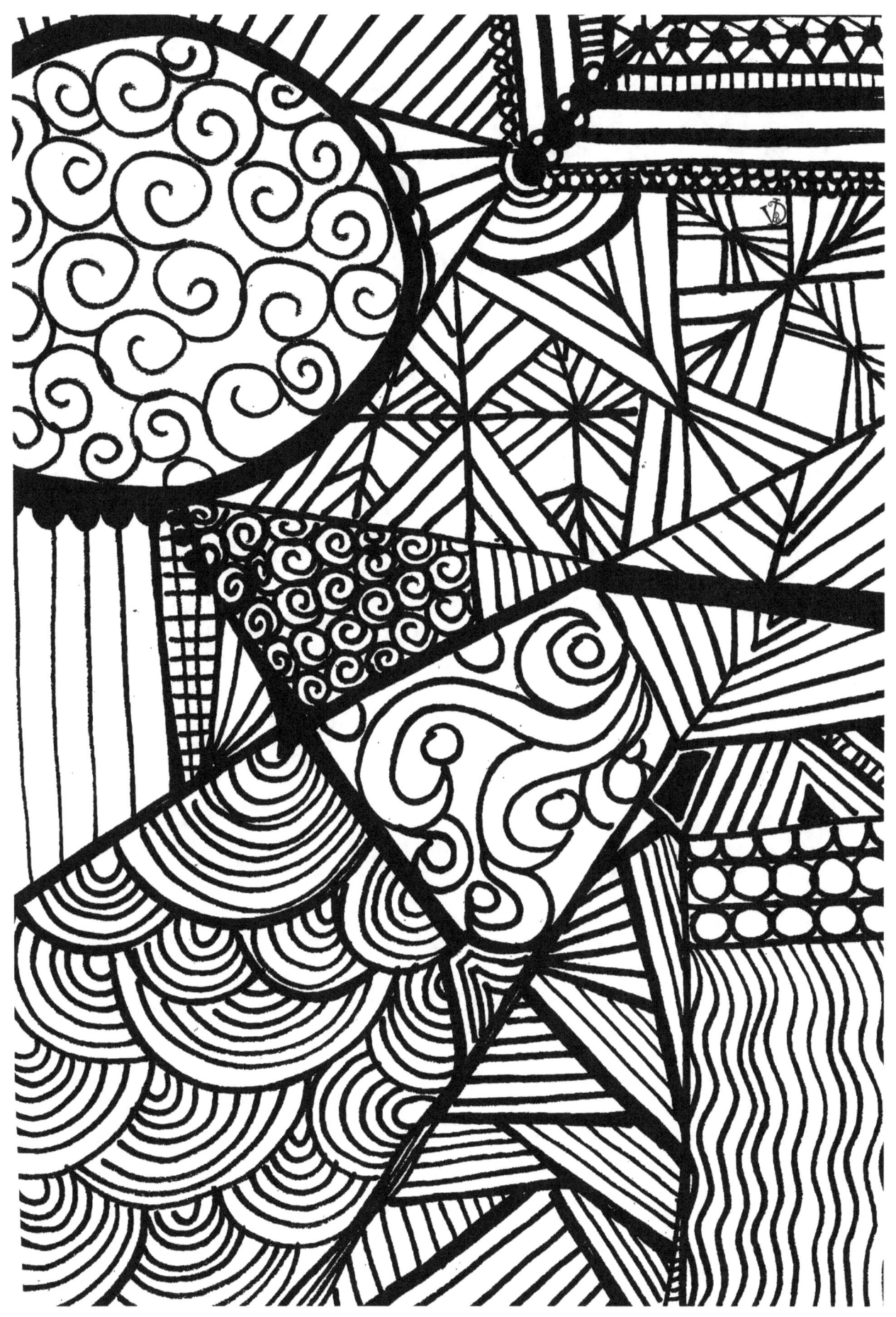

Abstract Expressions by Valerie Dowdy

Abstract Expressions by Valerie Dowdy

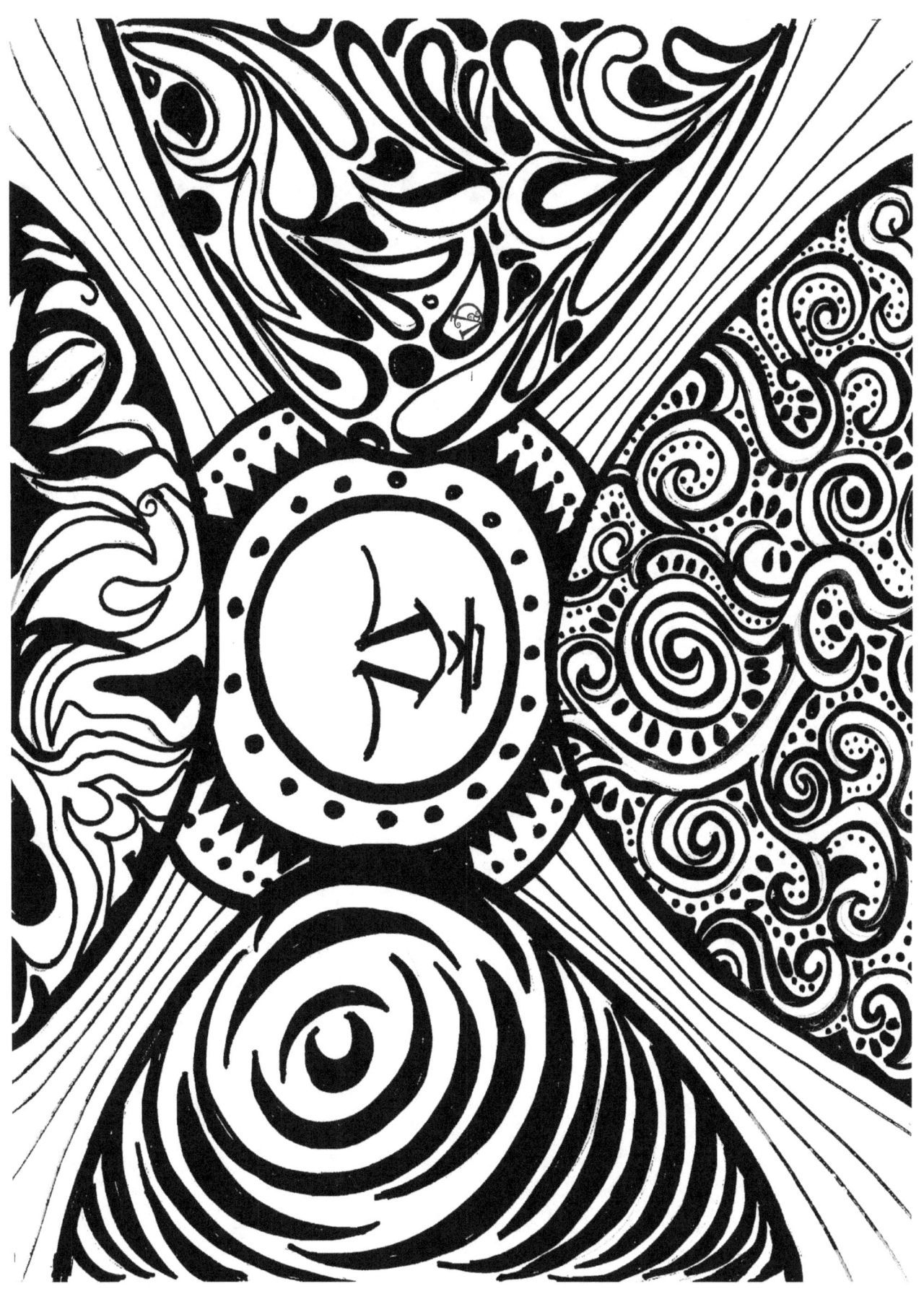

Abstract Expressions by Valerie Dowdy

Abstract Expressions by Valerie Dowdy

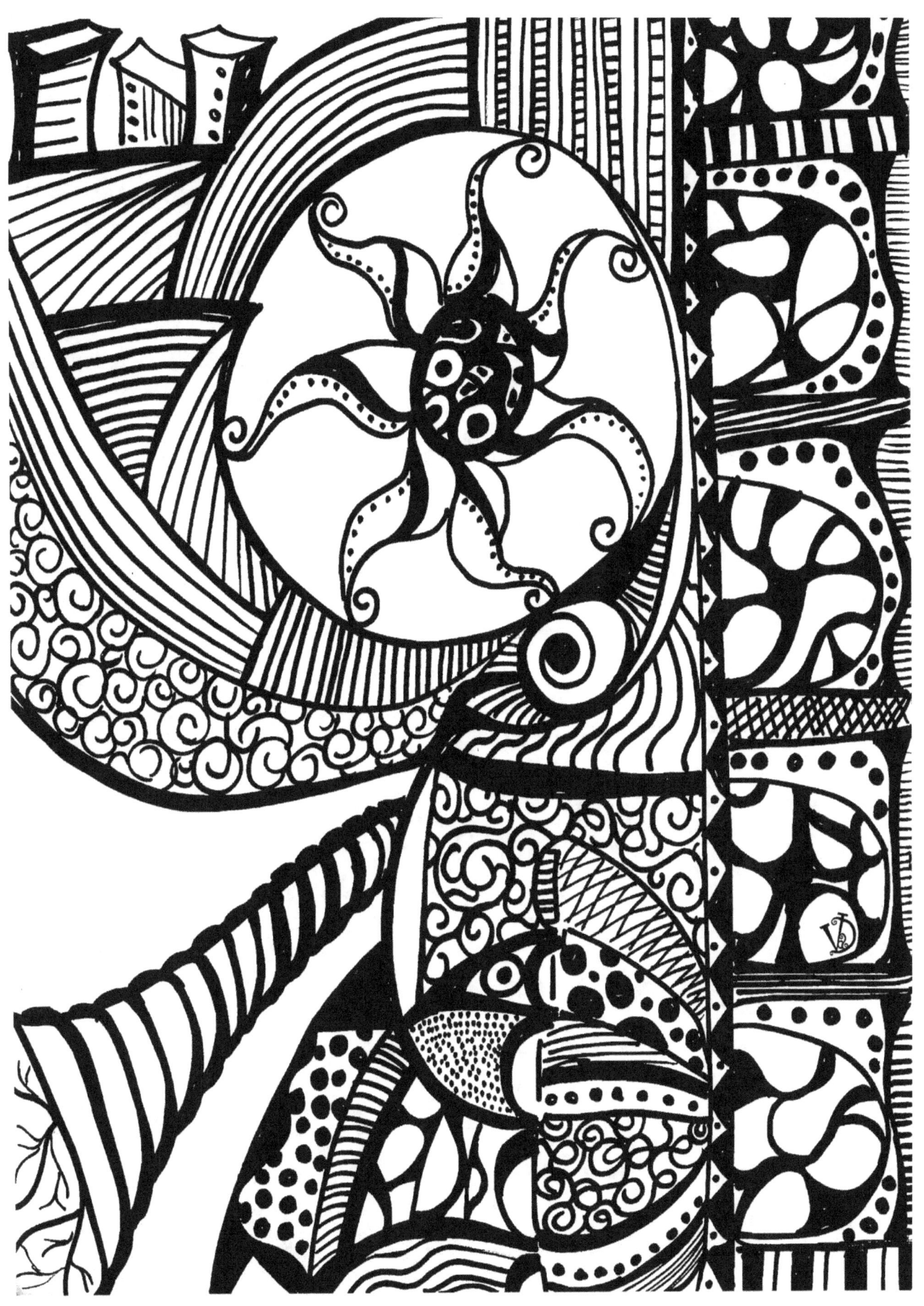

Abstract Expressions by Valerie Dowdy

Abstract Expressions by Valerie Dowdy

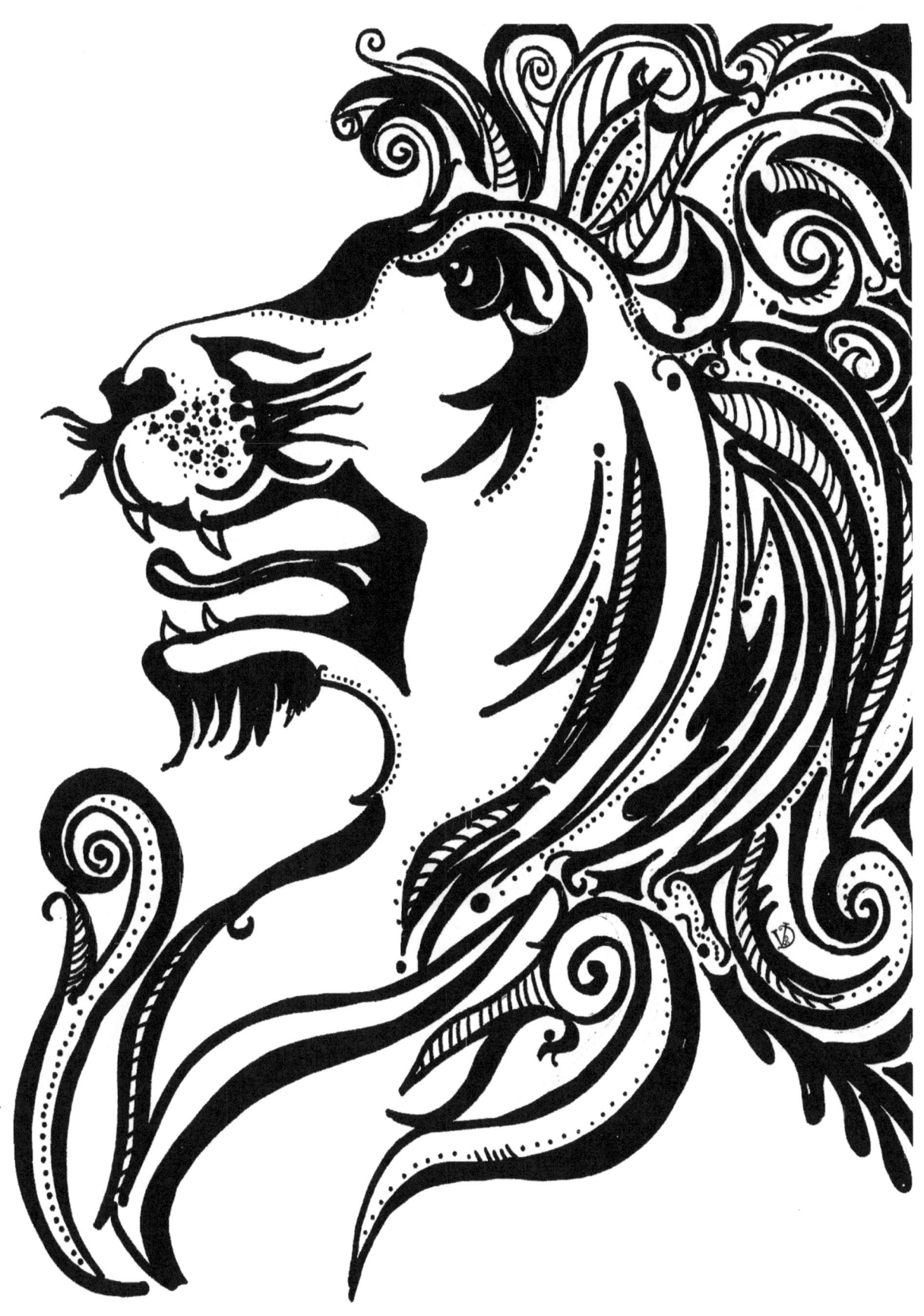

Abstract Expressions by Valerie Dowdy

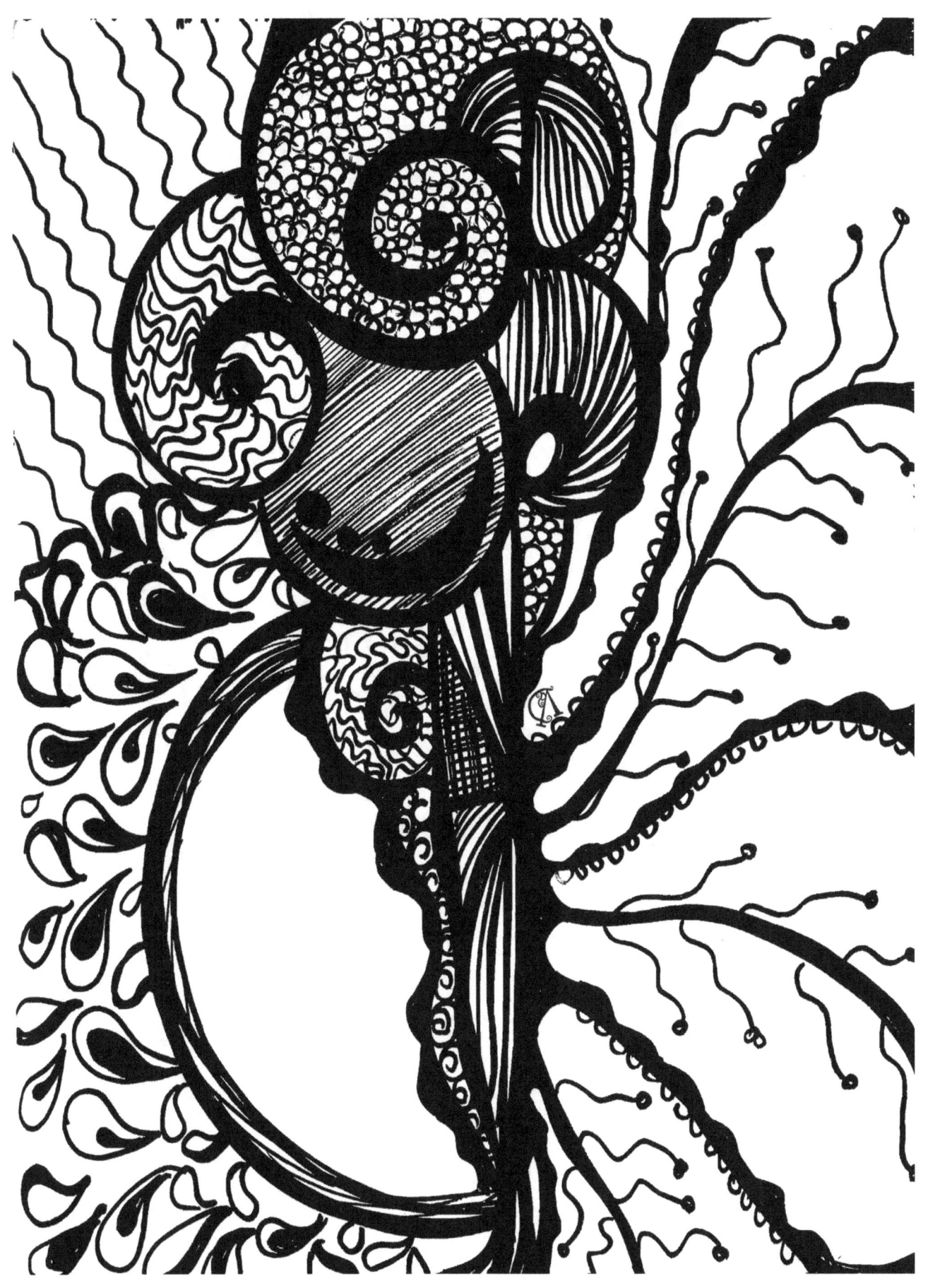

Abstract Expressions by Valerie Dowdy

Abstract Expressions by Valerie Dowdy

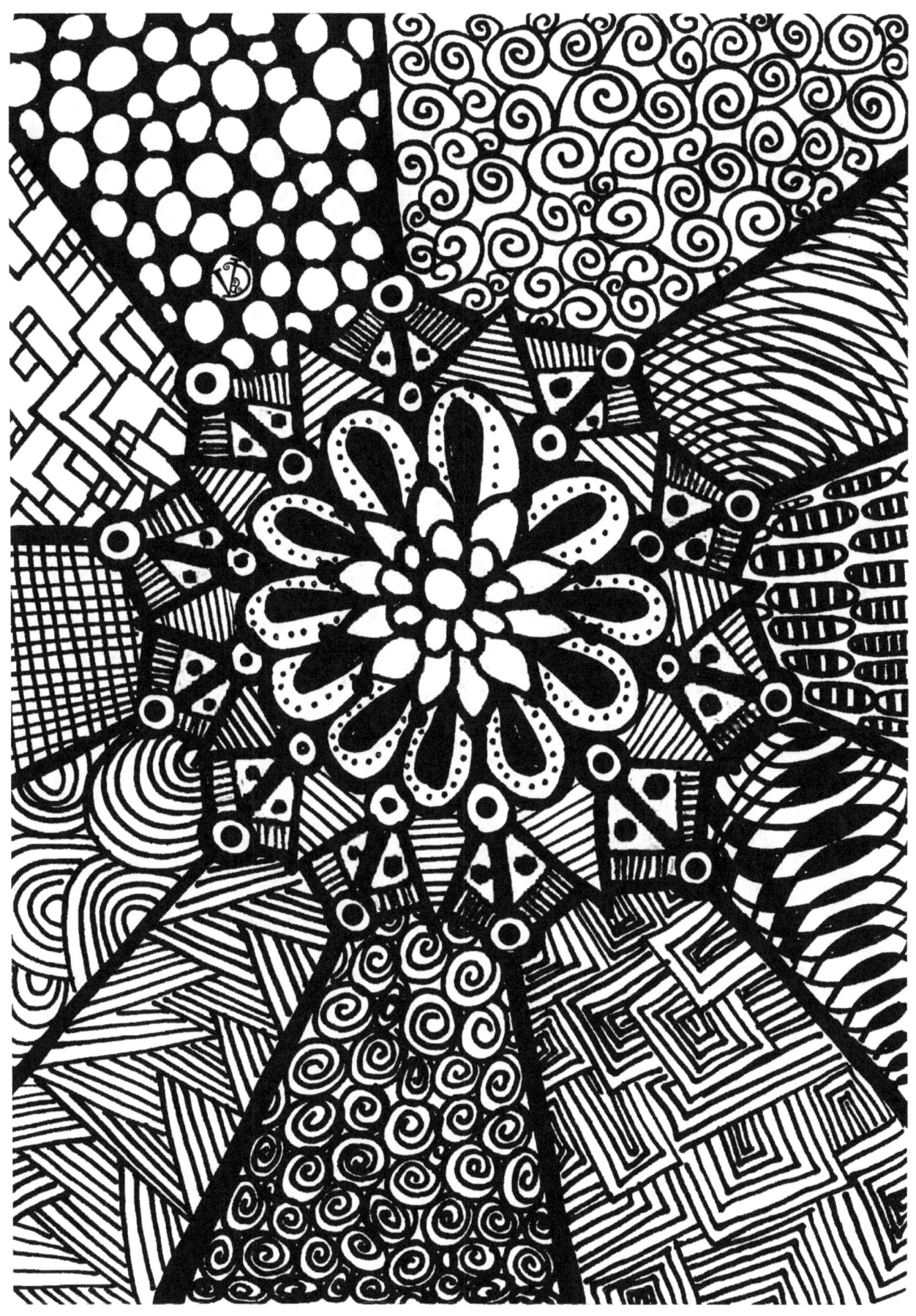

Abstract Expressions by Valerie Dowdy

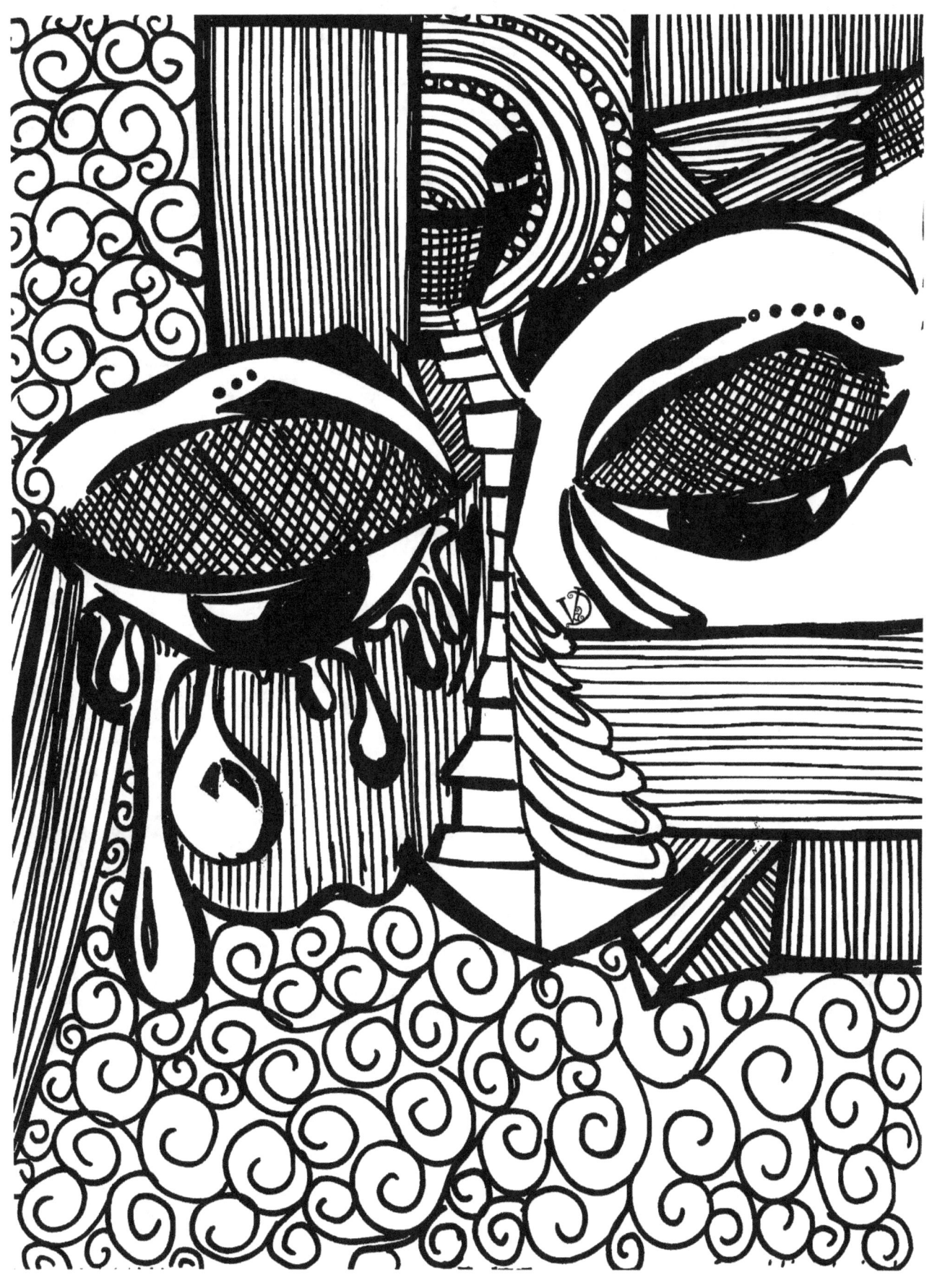

Abstract Expressions by Valerie Dowdy

Abstract Expressions by Valerie Dowdy

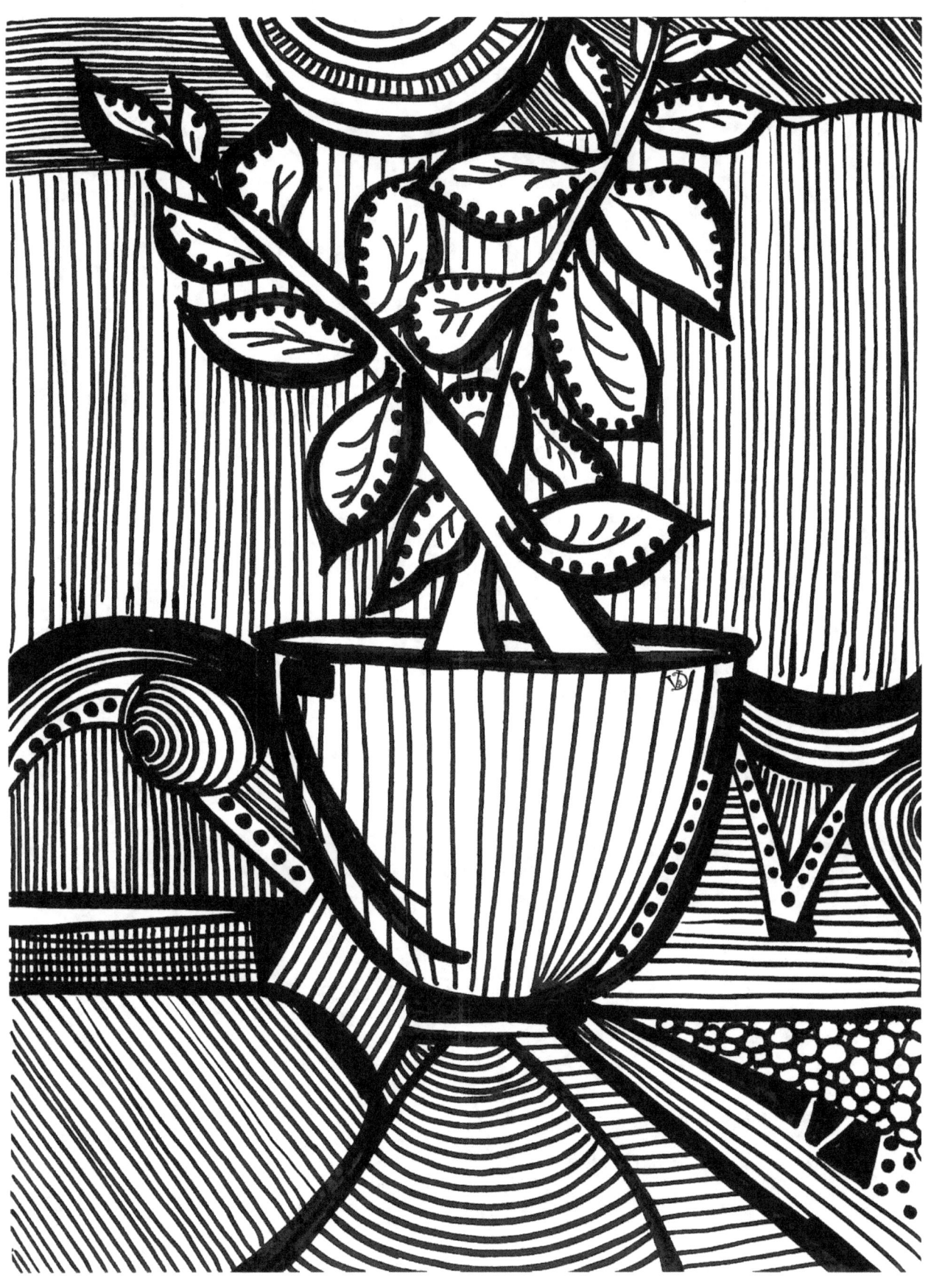

Abstract Expressions by Valerie Dowdy

Abstract Expressions by Valerie Dowdy

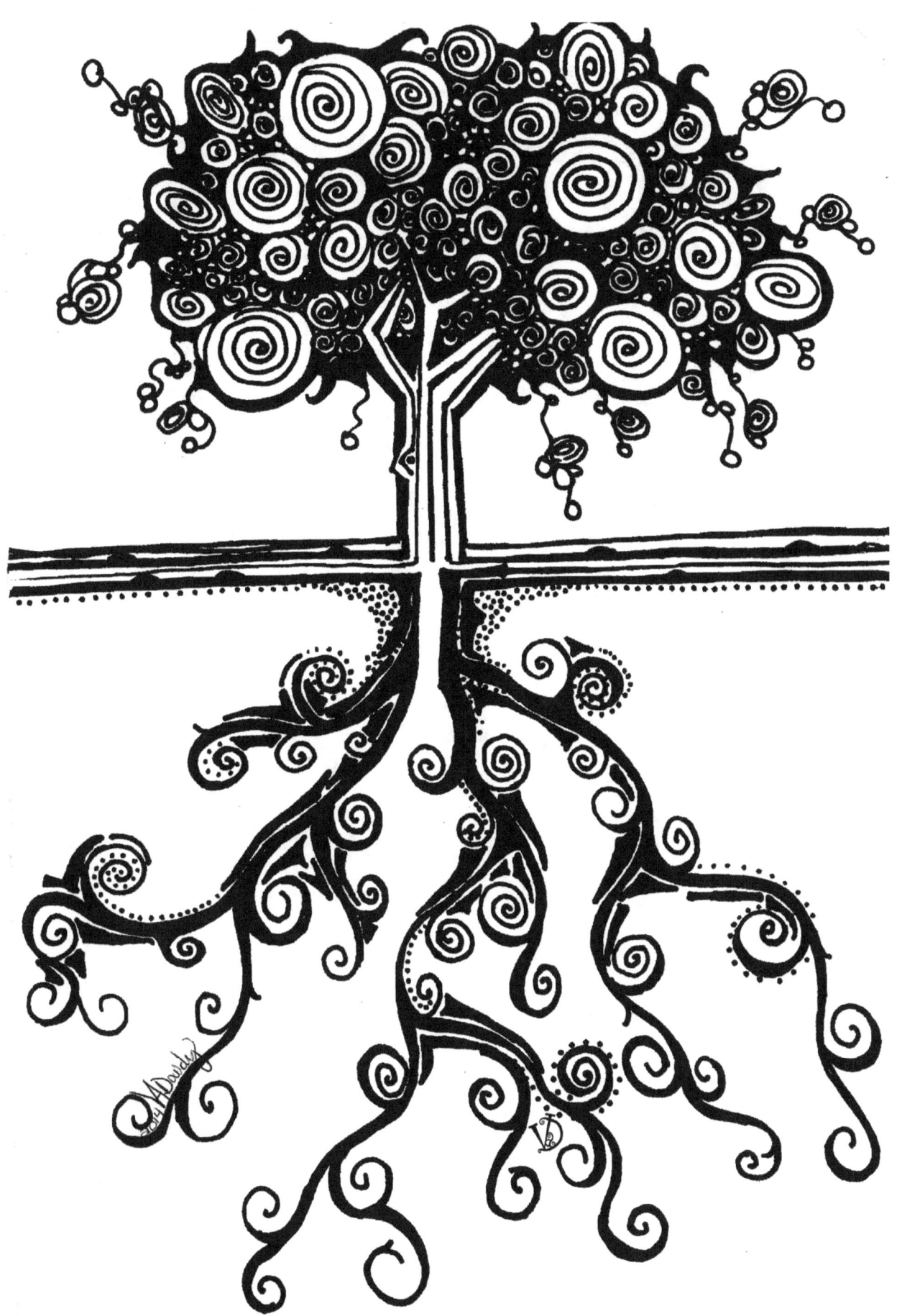

Abstract Expressions by Valerie Dowdy

Abstract Expressions by Valerie Dowdy

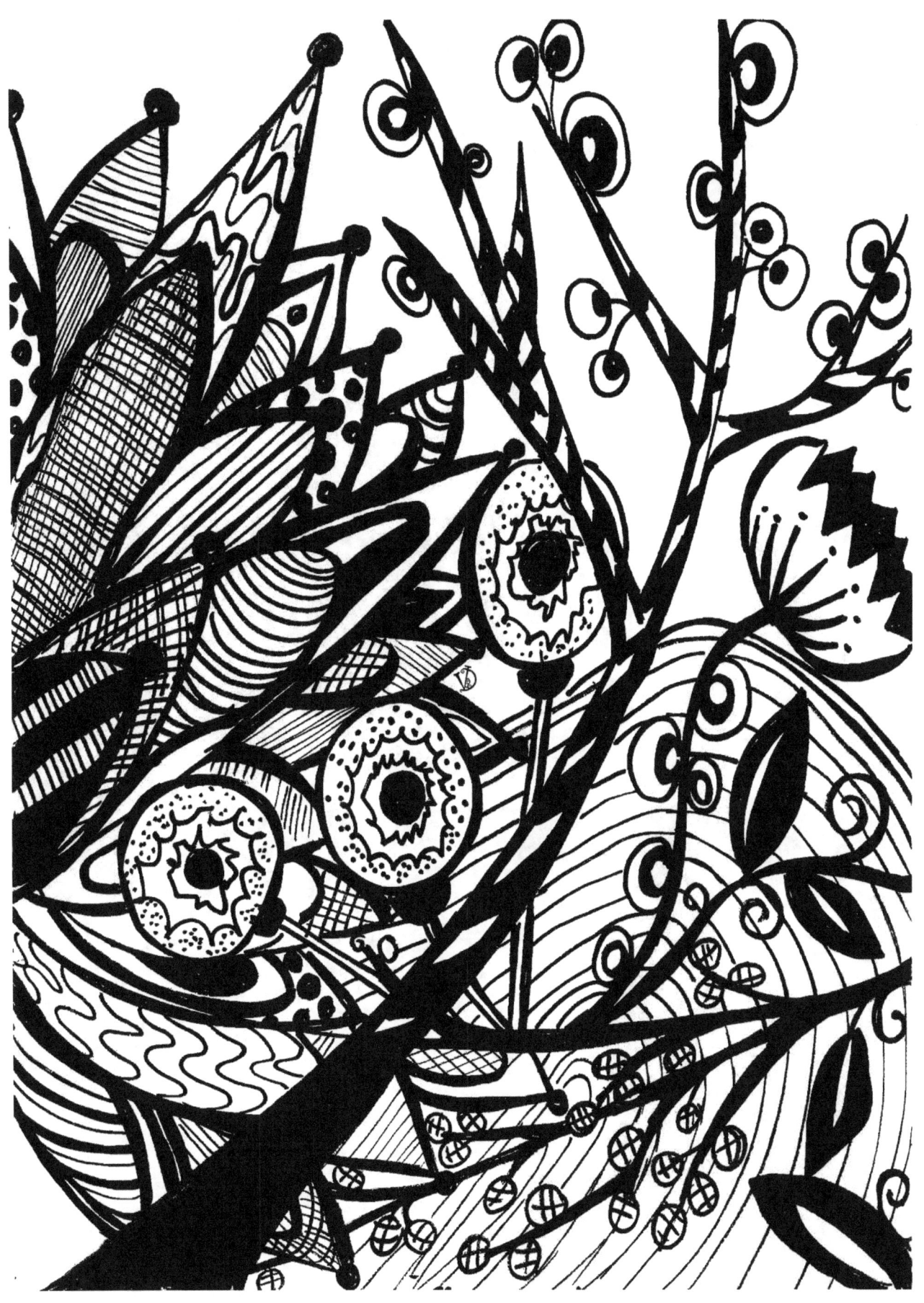

Abstract Expressions by Valerie Dowdy

Abstract Expressions by Valerie Dowdy

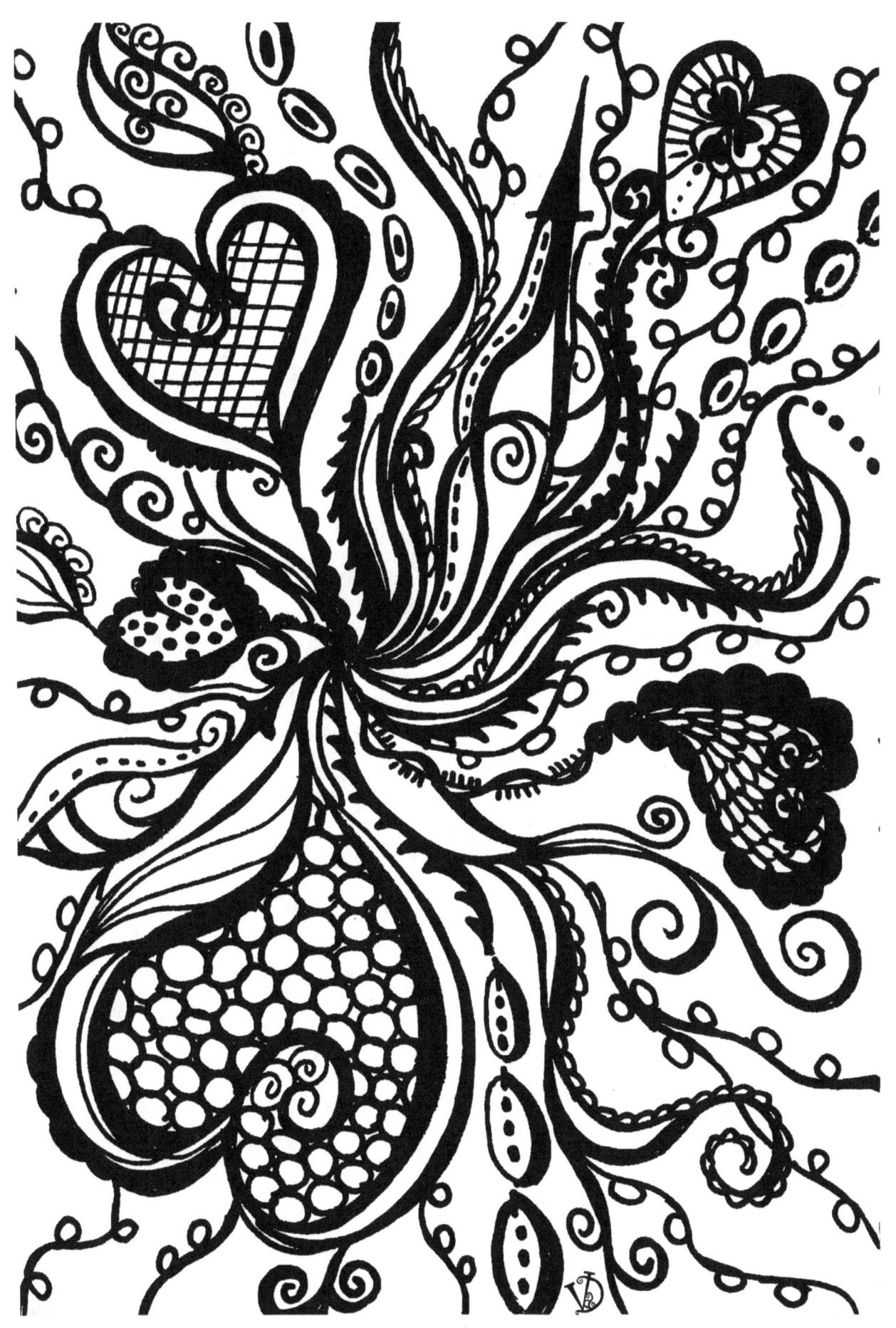

Abstract Expressions by Valerie Dowdy

Abstract Expressions by Valerie Dowdy

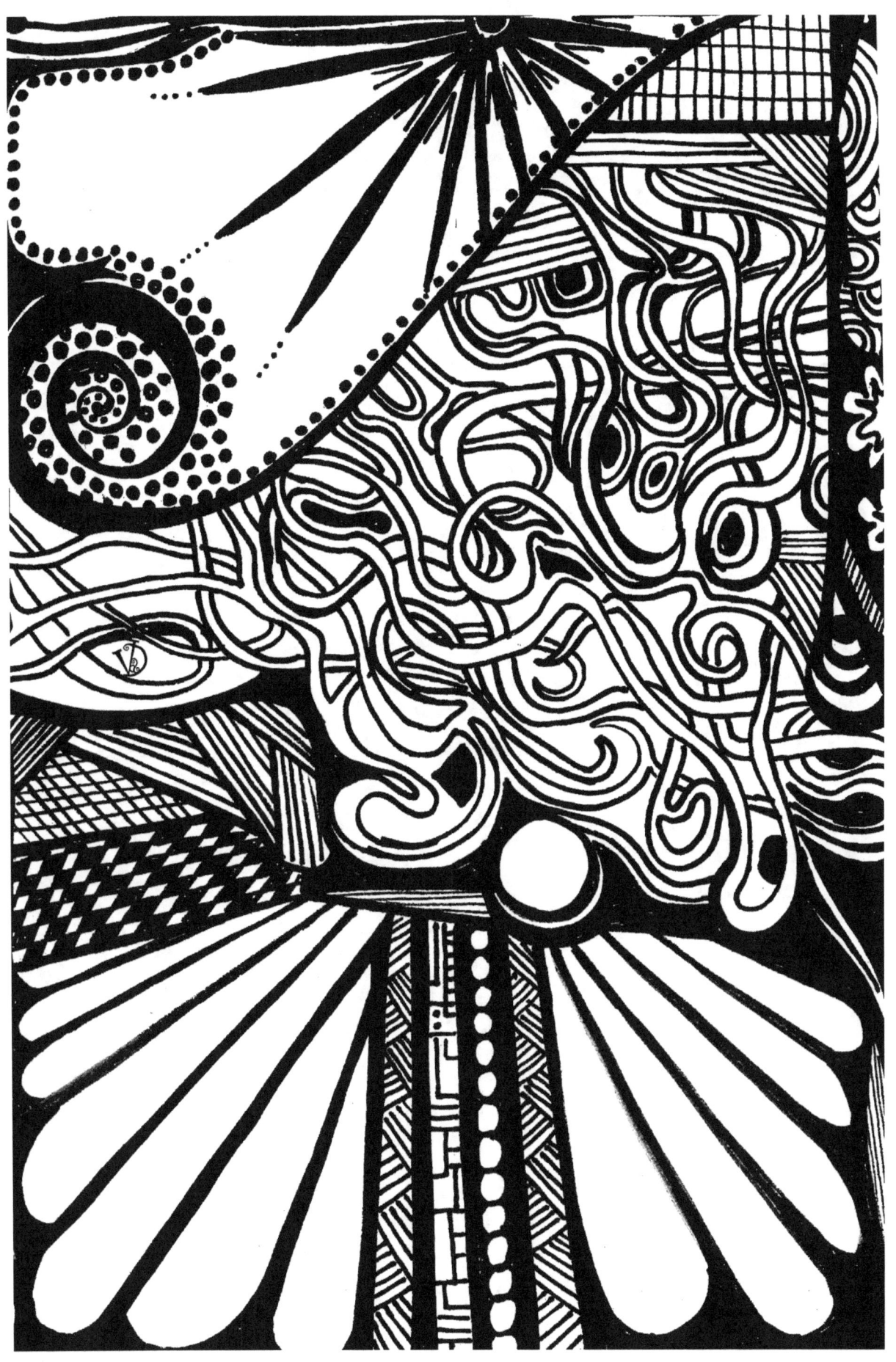

Abstract Expressions by Valerie Dowdy

Abstract Expressions by Valerie Dowdy

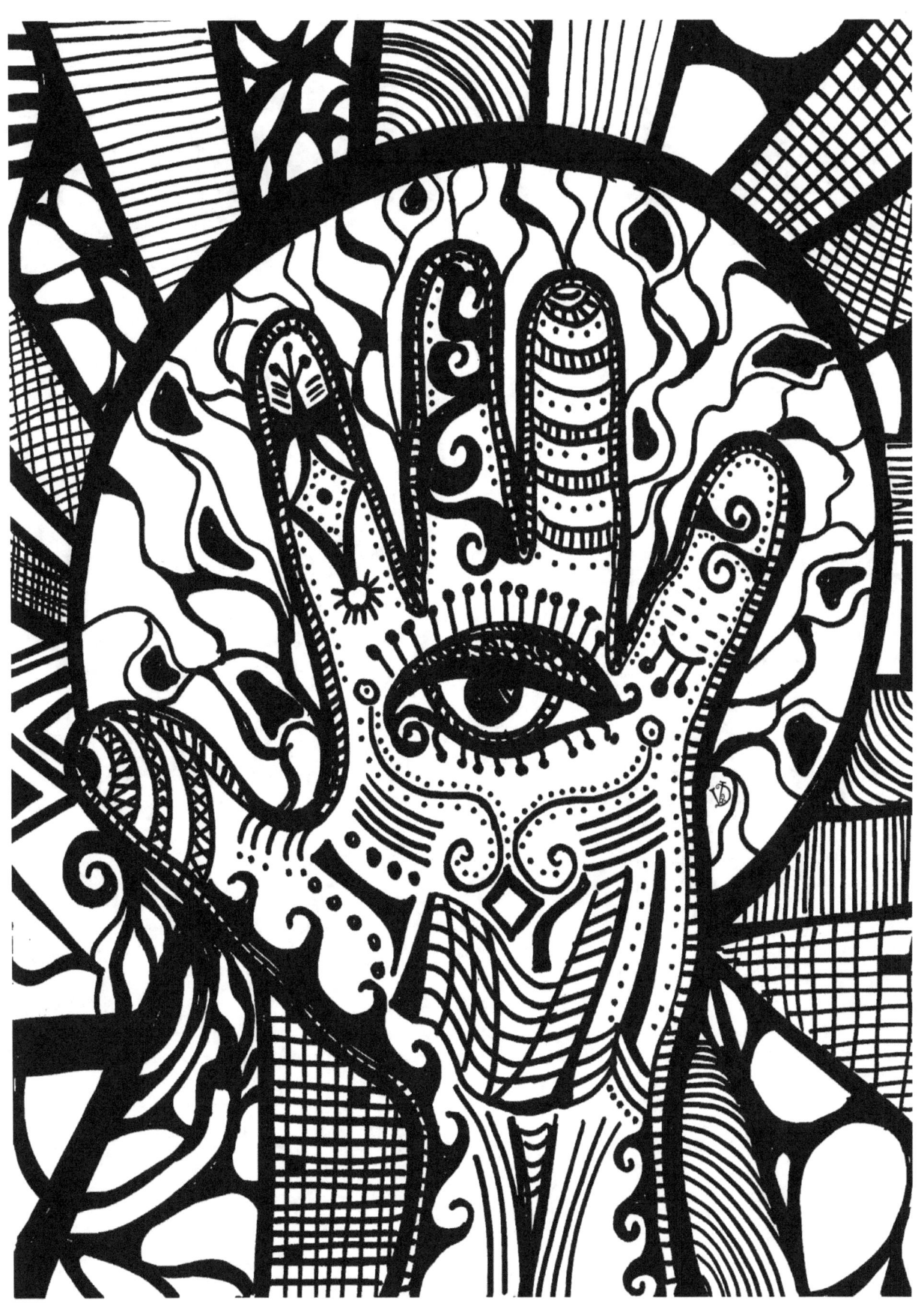

Abstract Expressions by Valerie Dowdy

Abstract Expressions by Valerie Dowdy

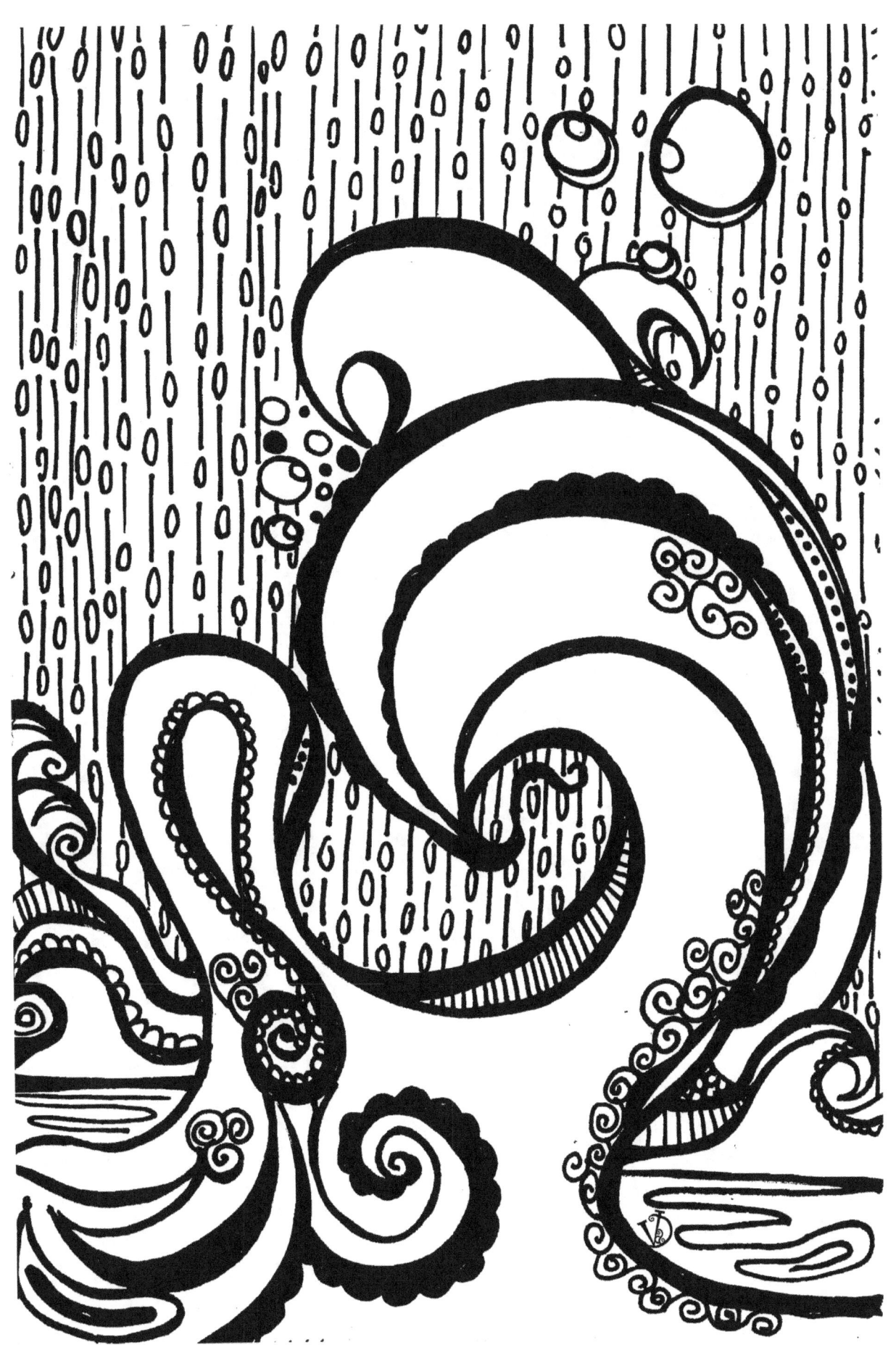

Abstract Expressions by Valerie Dowdy

Abstract Expressions by Valerie Dowdy

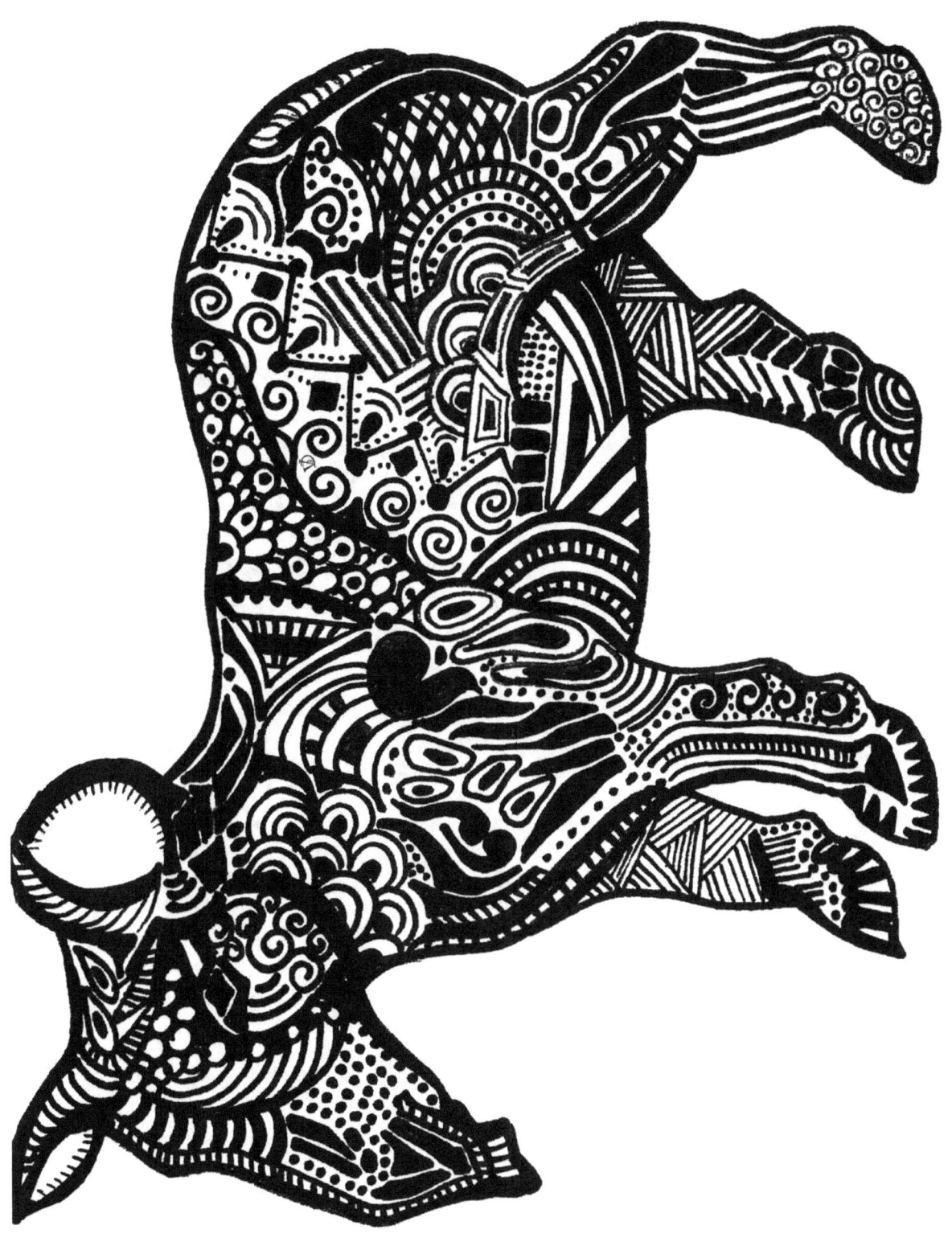

Abstract Expressions by Valerie Dowdy

Abstract Expressions by Valerie Dowdy

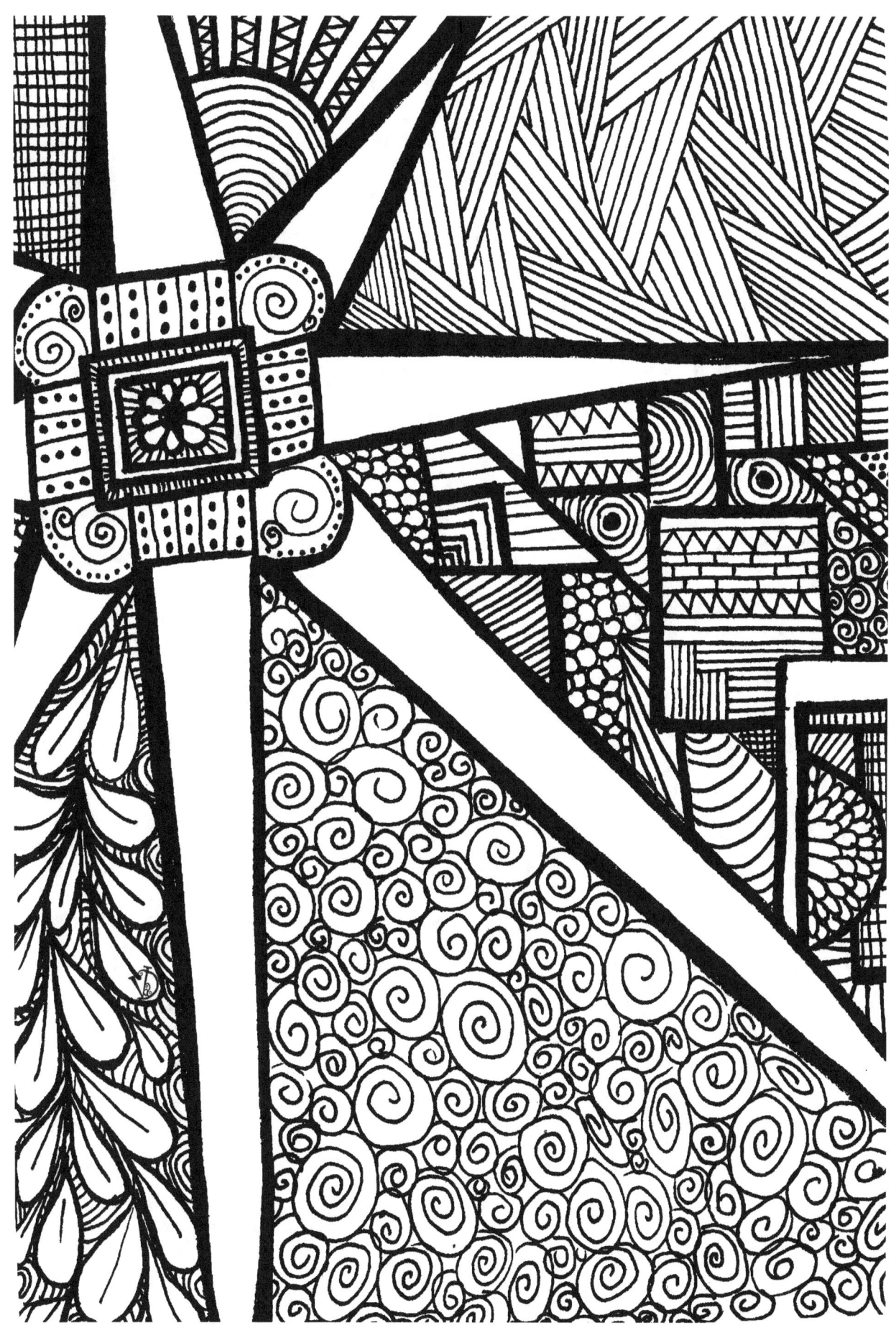

Abstract Expressions by Valerie Dowdy

Abstract Expressions by Valerie Dowdy

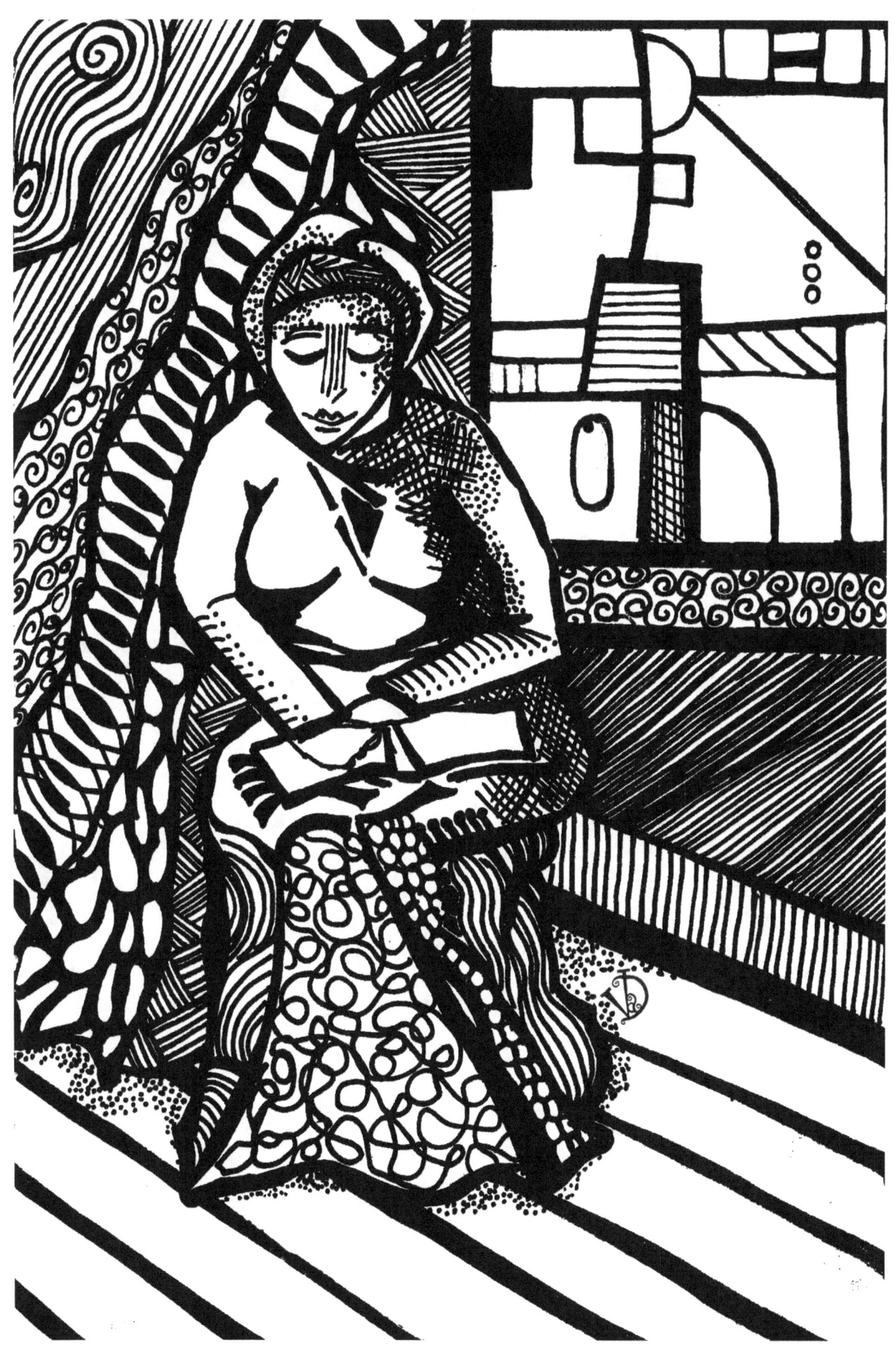

Abstract Expressions by Valerie Dowdy

Abstract Expressions by Valerie Dowdy

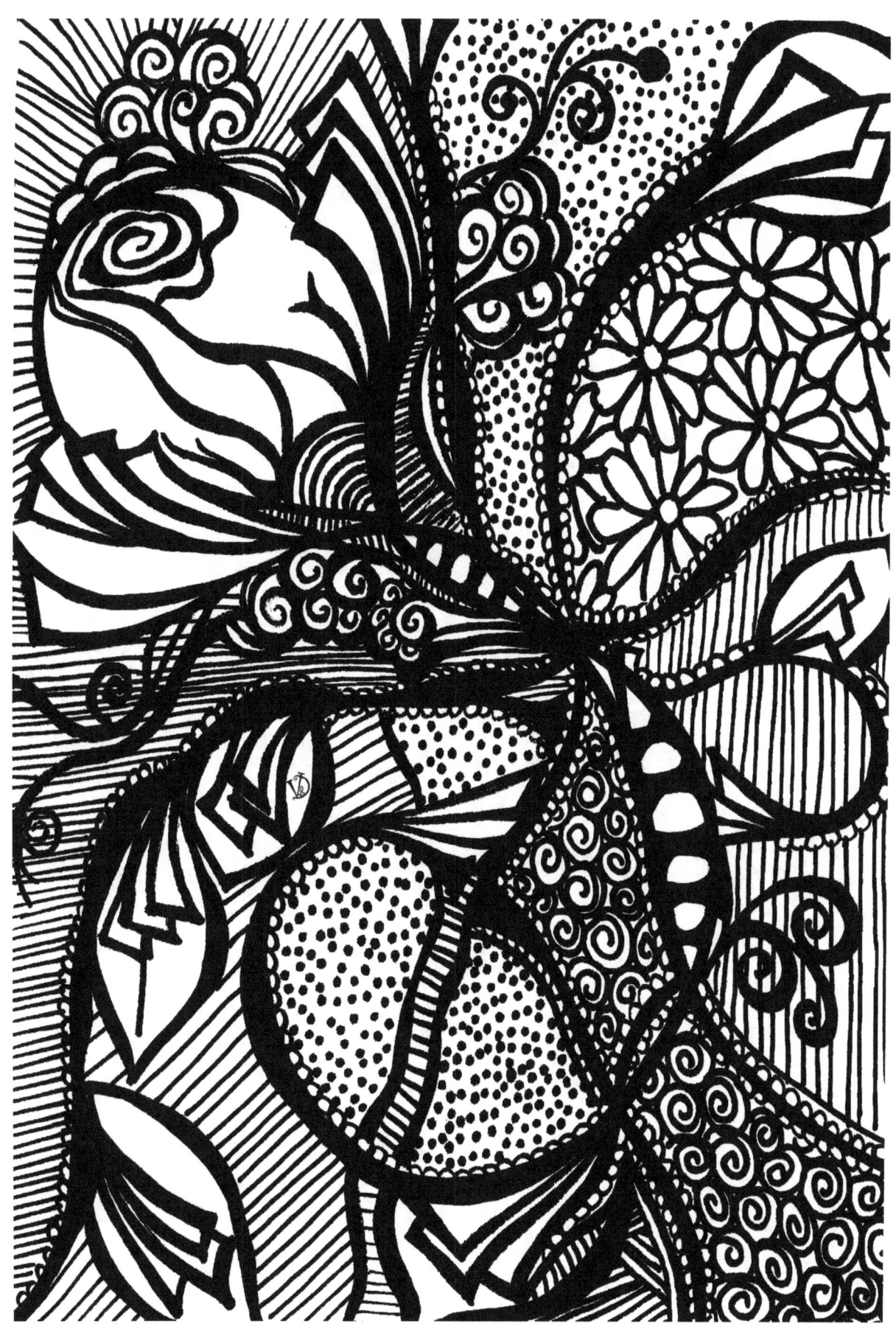

Abstract Expressions by Valerie Dowdy

Abstract Expressions by Valerie Dowdy

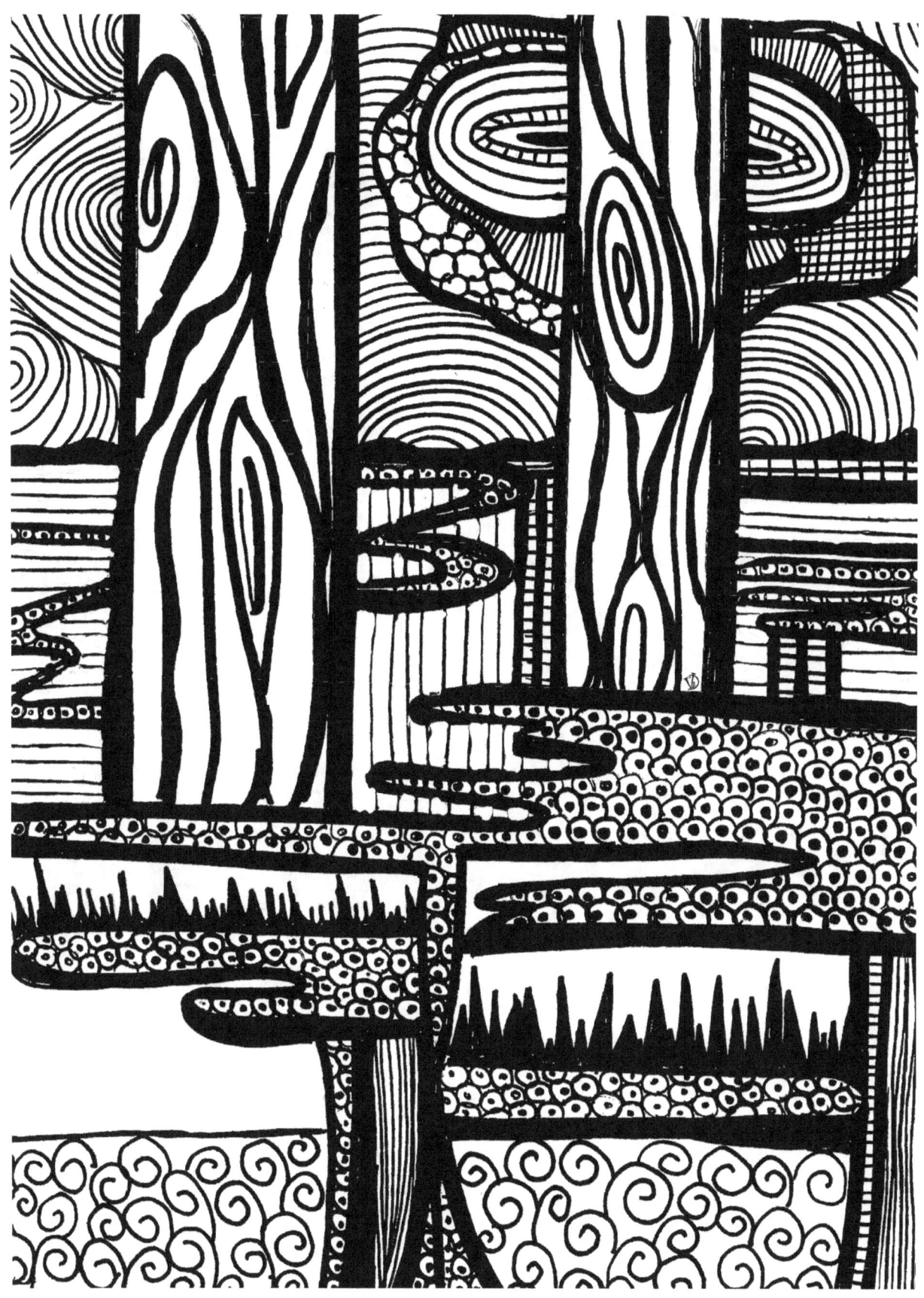

Abstract Expressions by Valerie Dowdy

Abstract Expressions by Valerie Dowdy

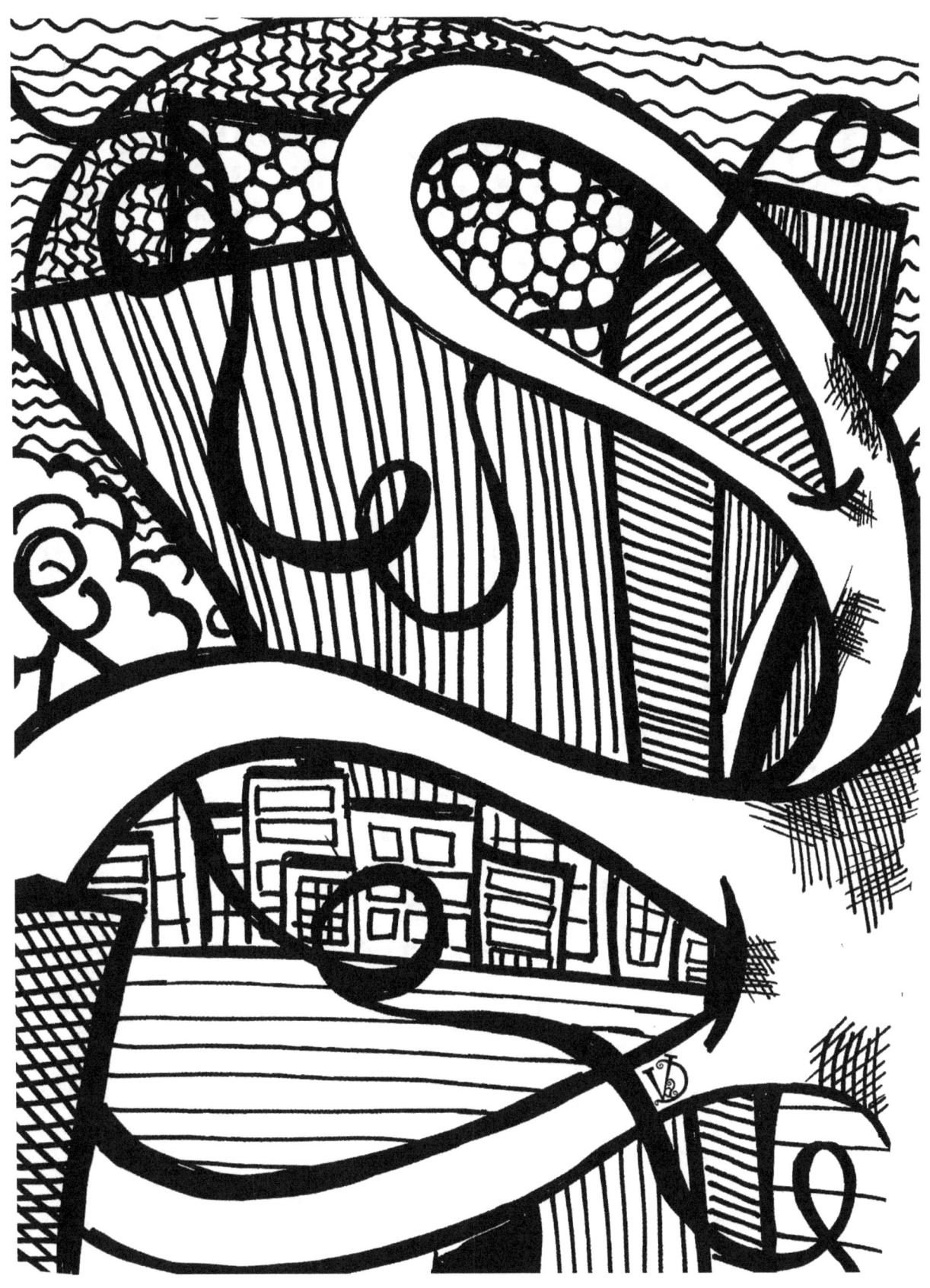

Abstract Expressions by Valerie Dowdy

Abstract Expressions by Valerie Dowdy

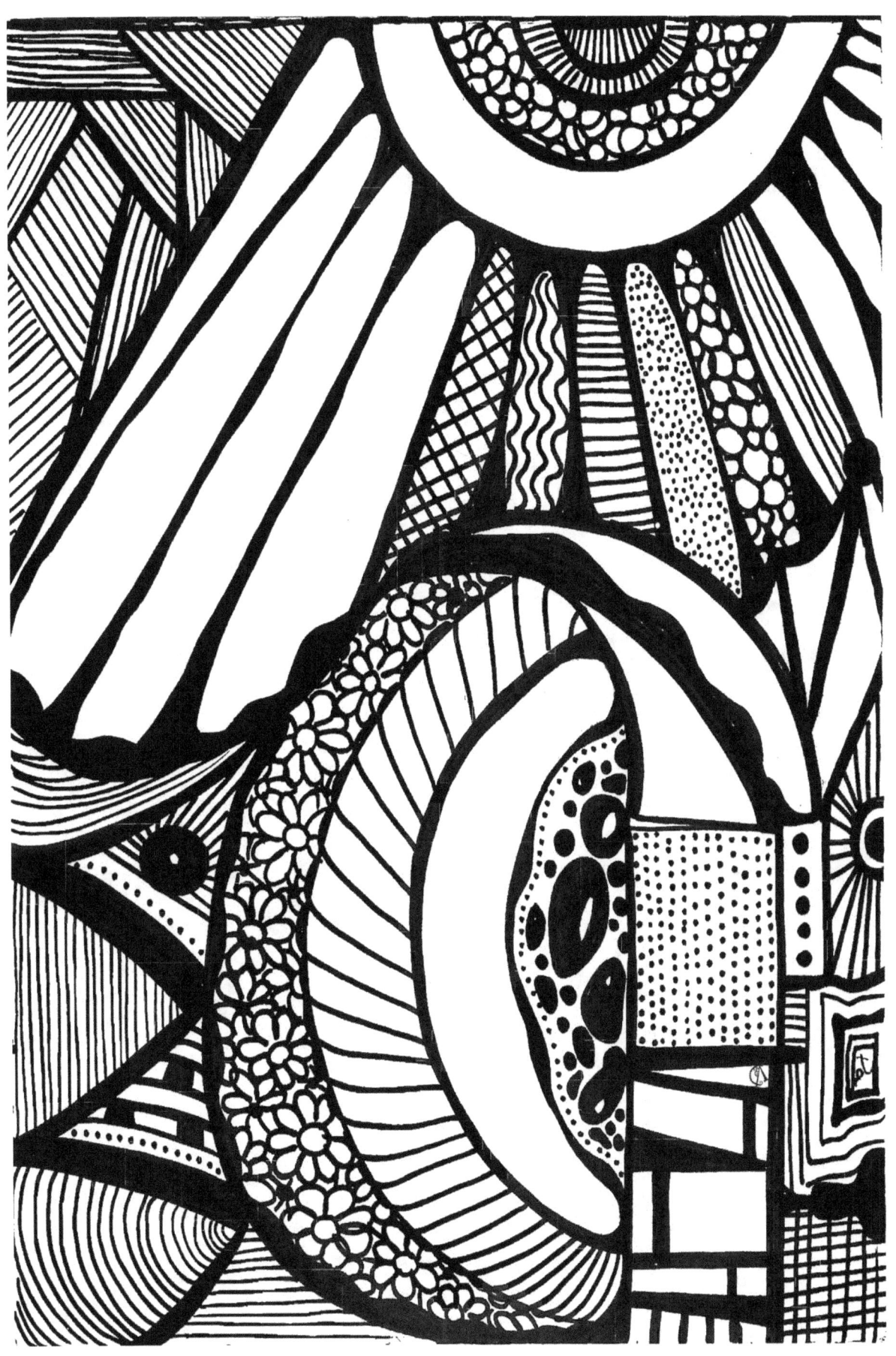

Abstract Expressions by Valerie Dowdy

Abstract Expressions by Valerie Dowdy

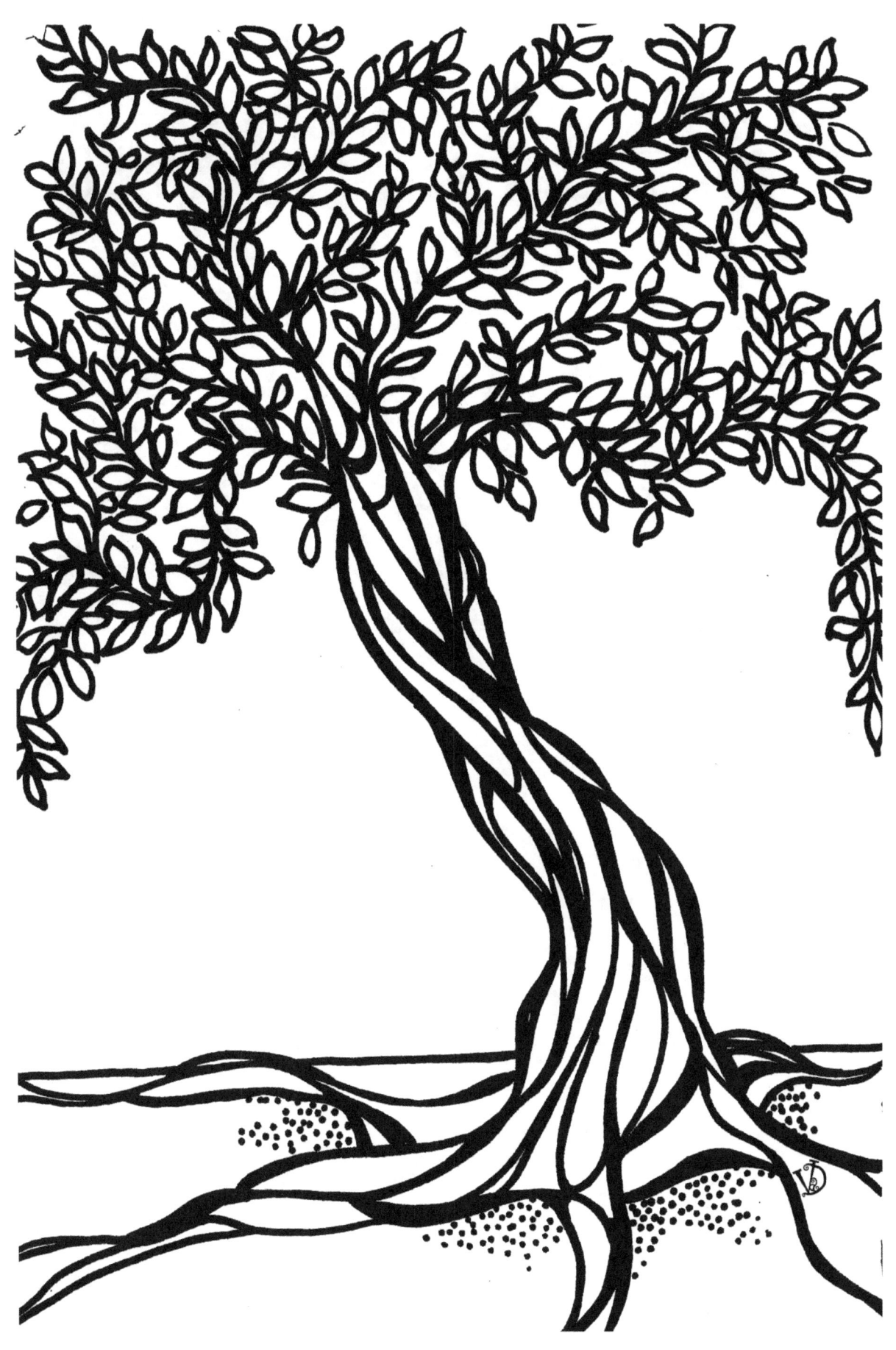

Abstract Expressions by Valerie Dowdy

Abstract Expressions by Valerie Dowdy

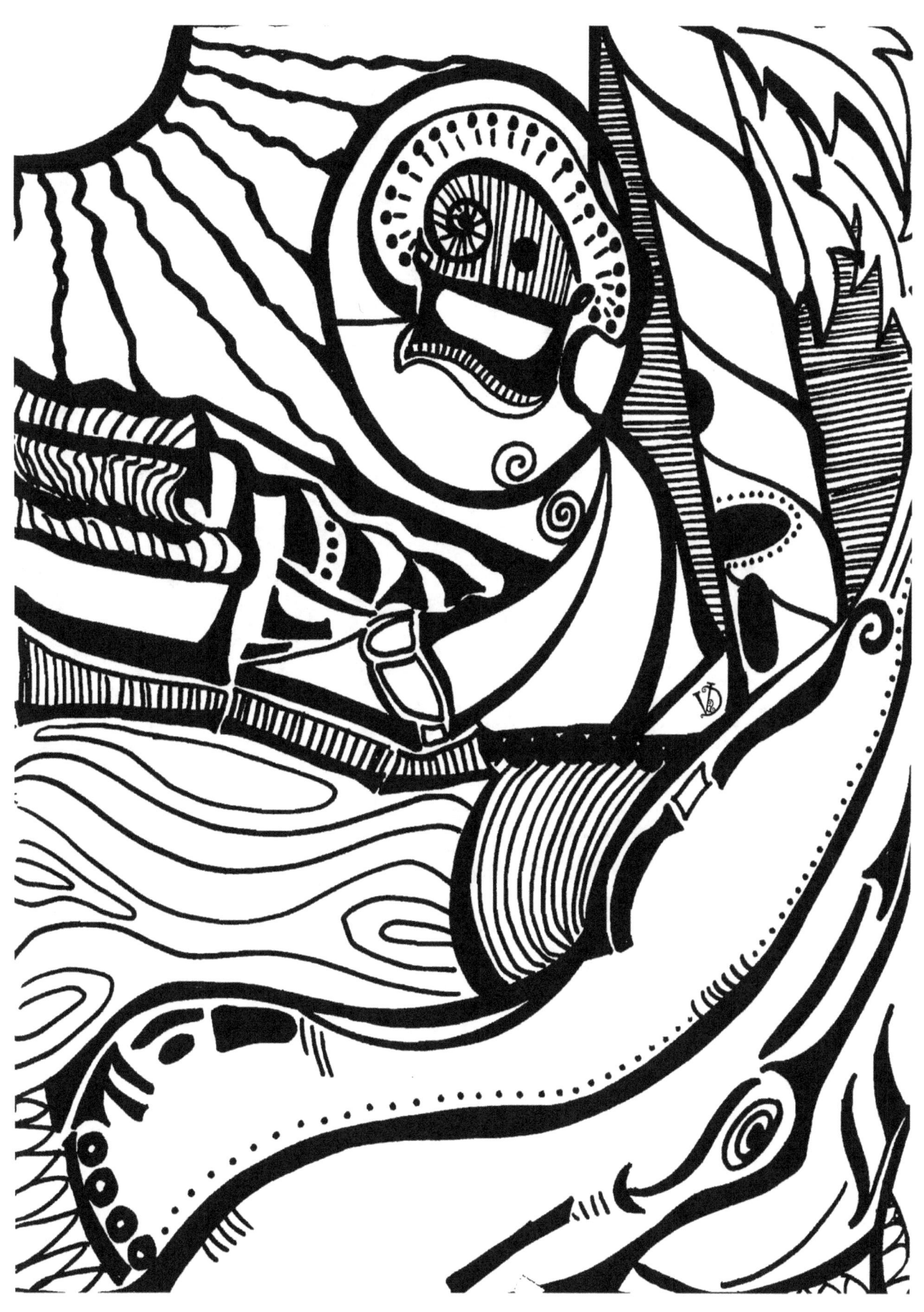

Abstract Expressions by Valerie Dowdy

Abstract Expressions by Valerie Dowdy

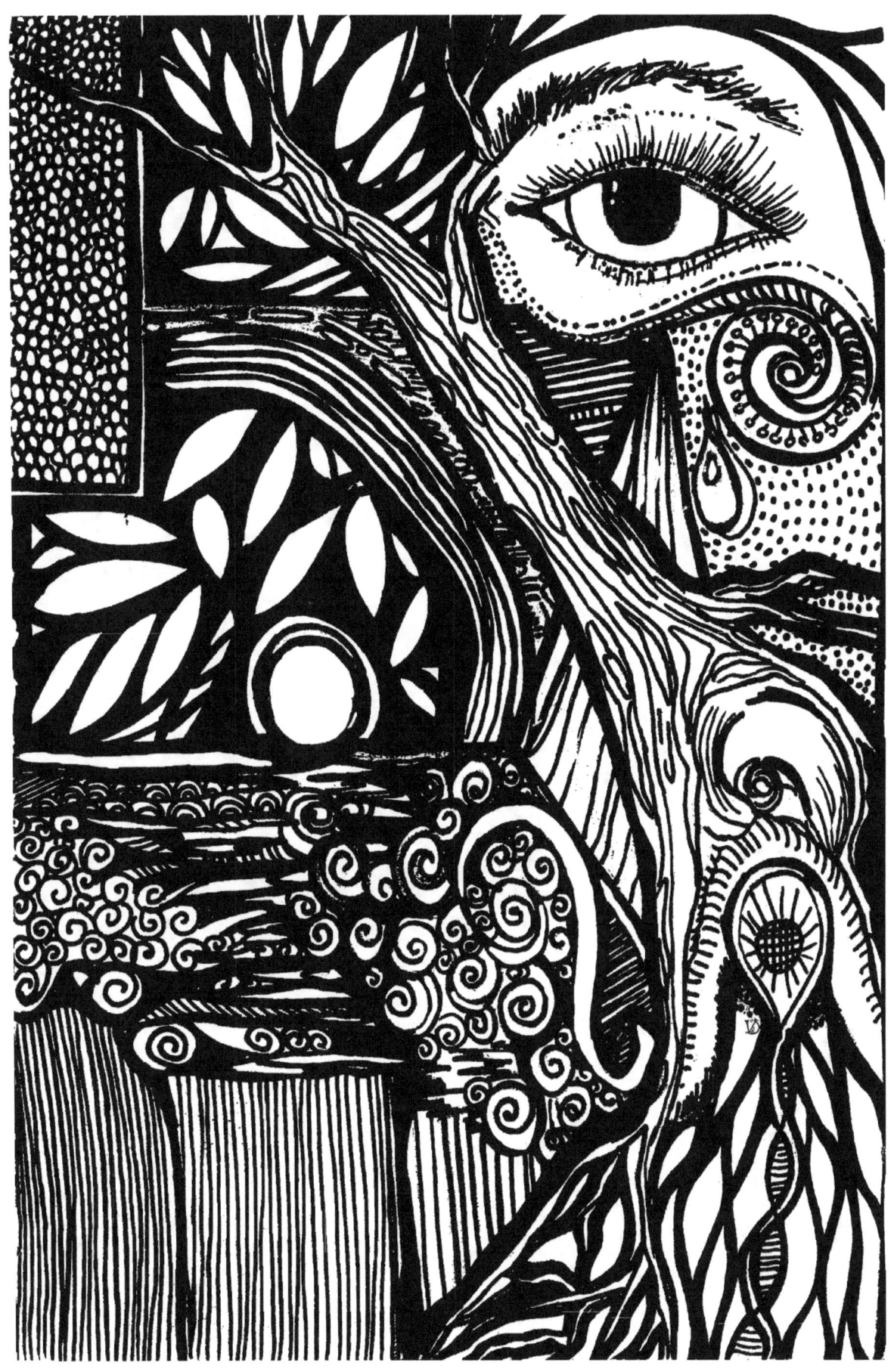

Abstract Expressions by Valerie Dowdy

Abstract Expressions by Valerie Dowdy

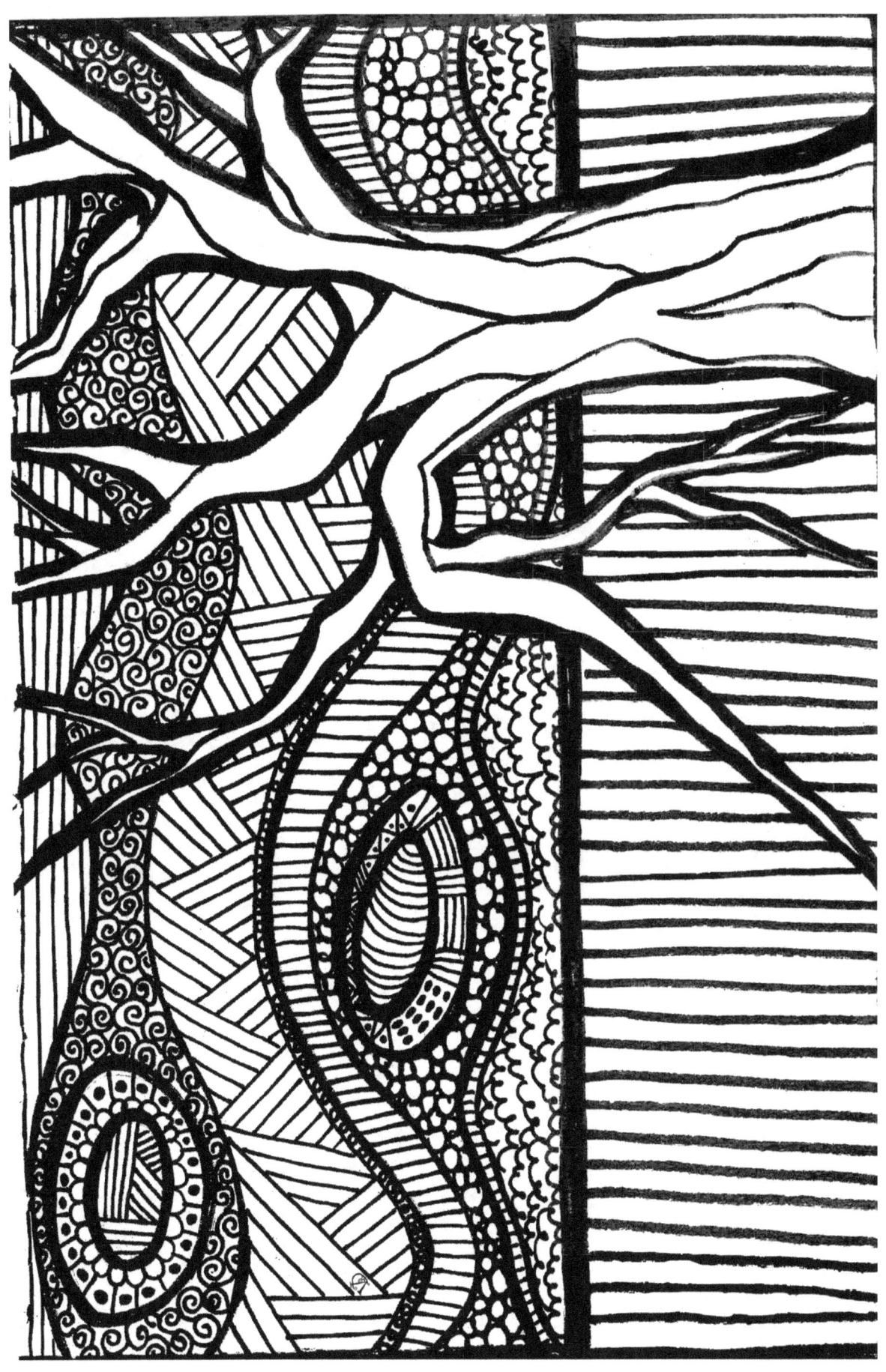

Abstract Expressions by Valerie Dowdy

Abstract Expressions by Valerie Dowdy

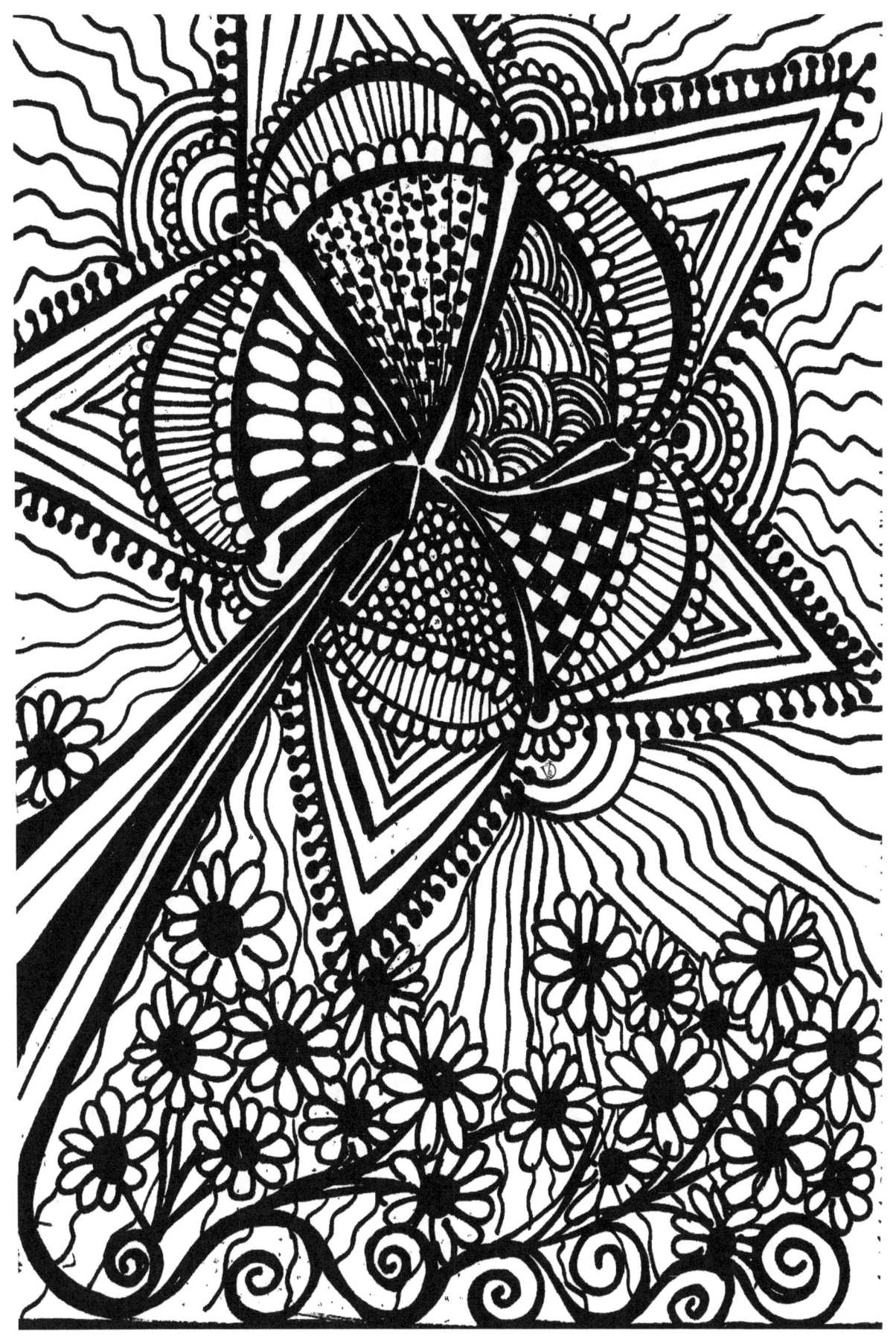

Abstract Expressions by Valerie Dowdy

Abstract Expressions by Valerie Dowdy

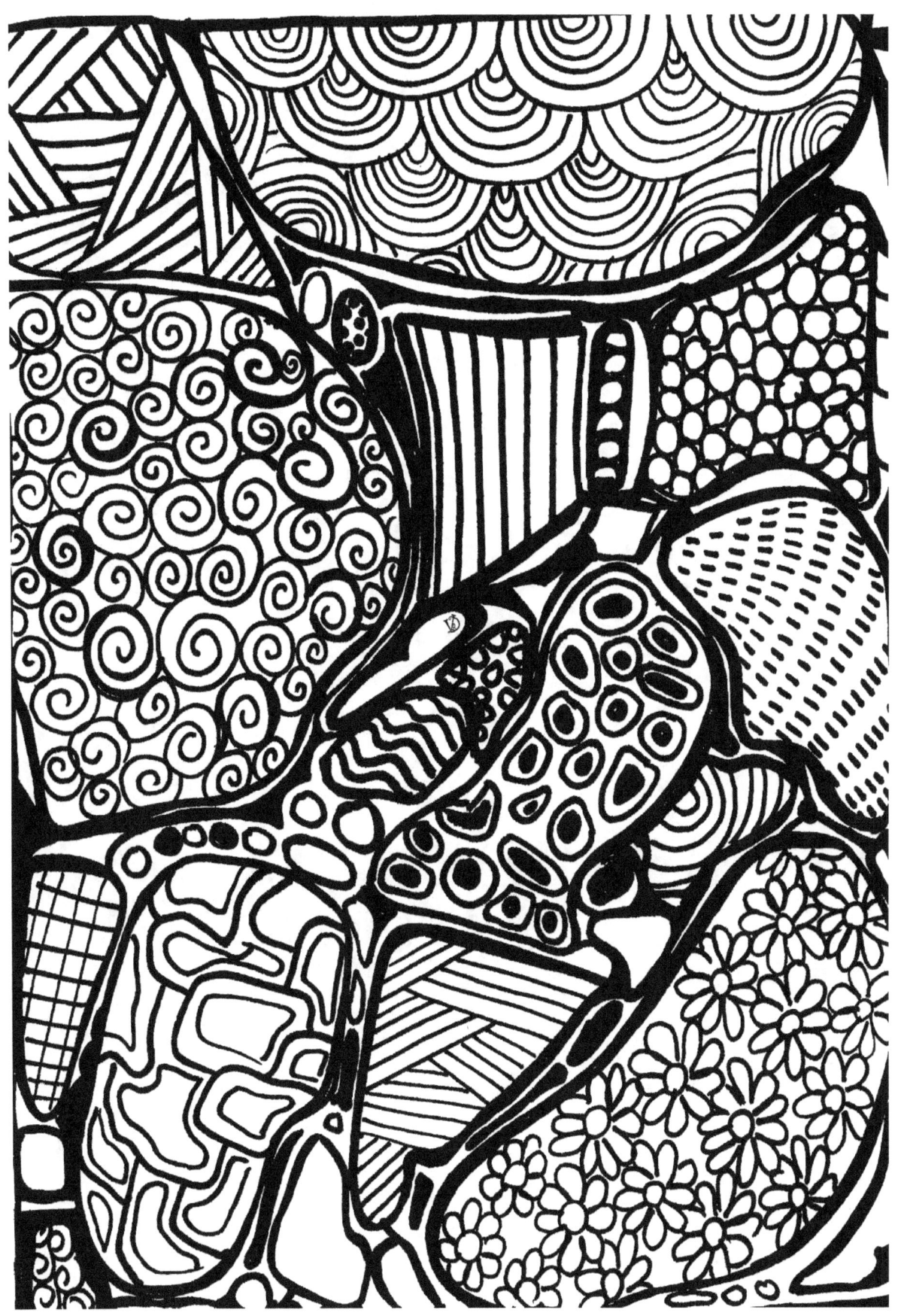

Abstract Expressions by Valerie Dowdy

Abstract Expressions by Valerie Dowdy

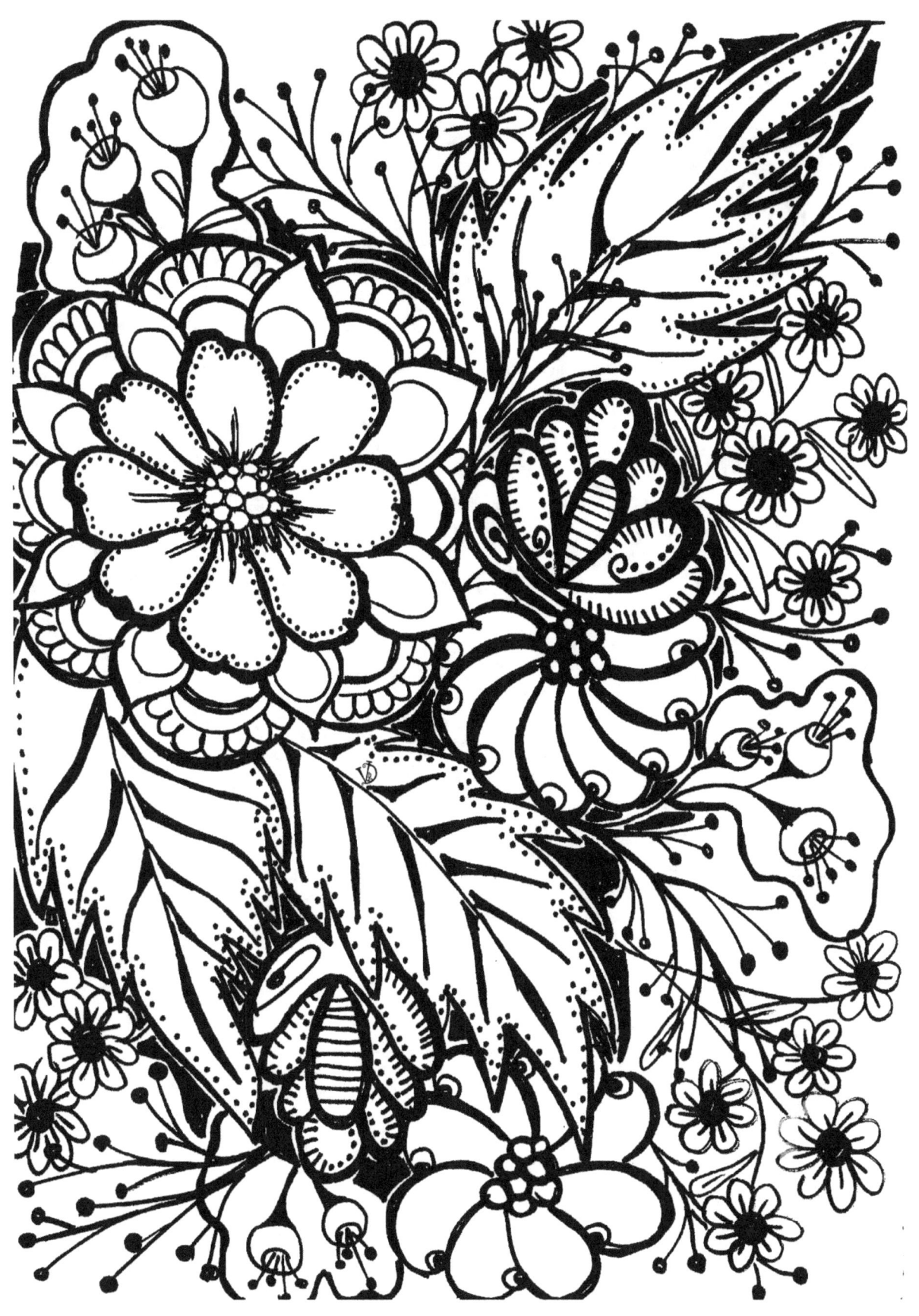

Abstract Expressions by Valerie Dowdy

Abstract Expressions by Valerie Dowdy

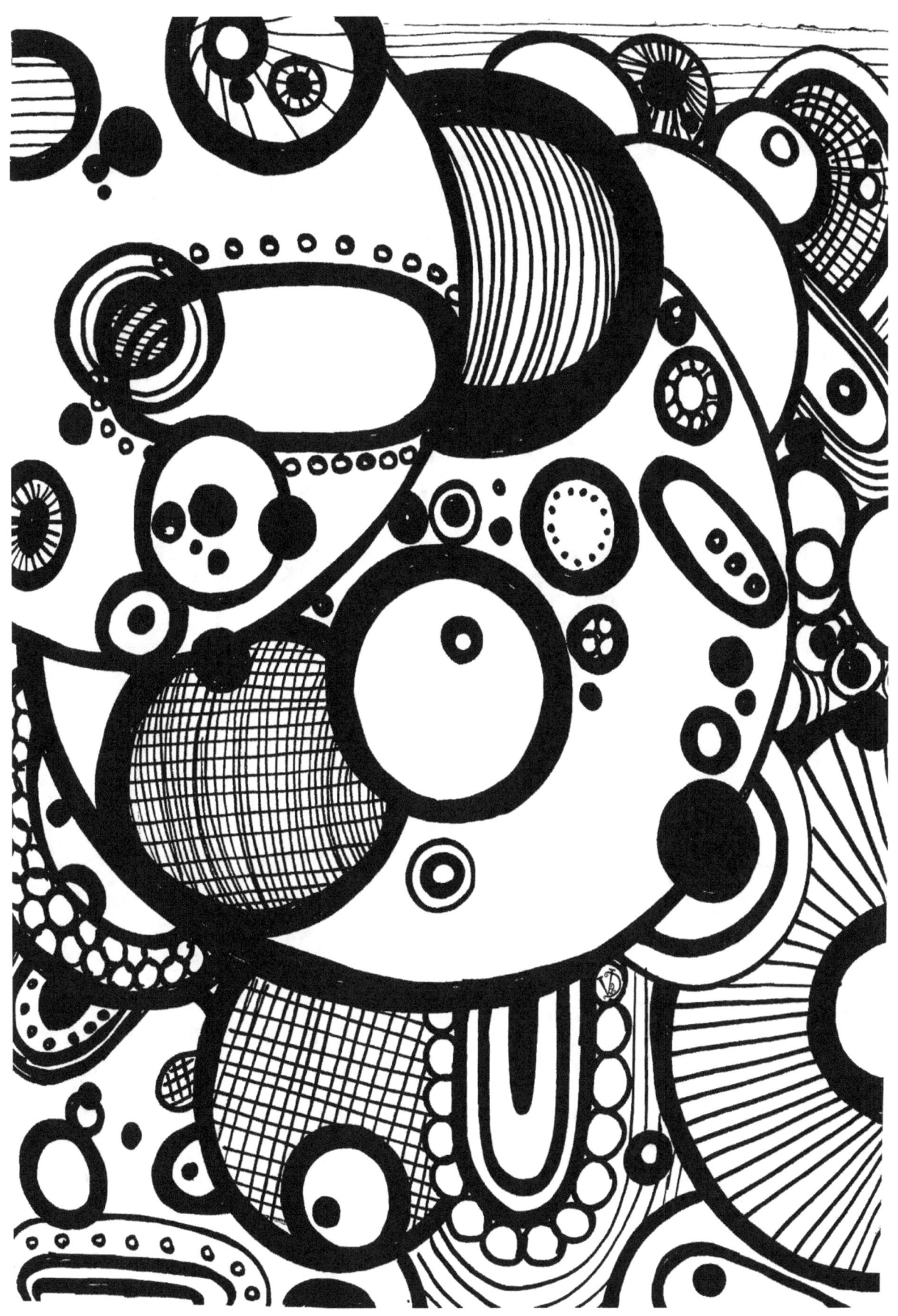

Abstract Expressions by Valerie Dowdy

Abstract Expressions by Valerie Dowdy

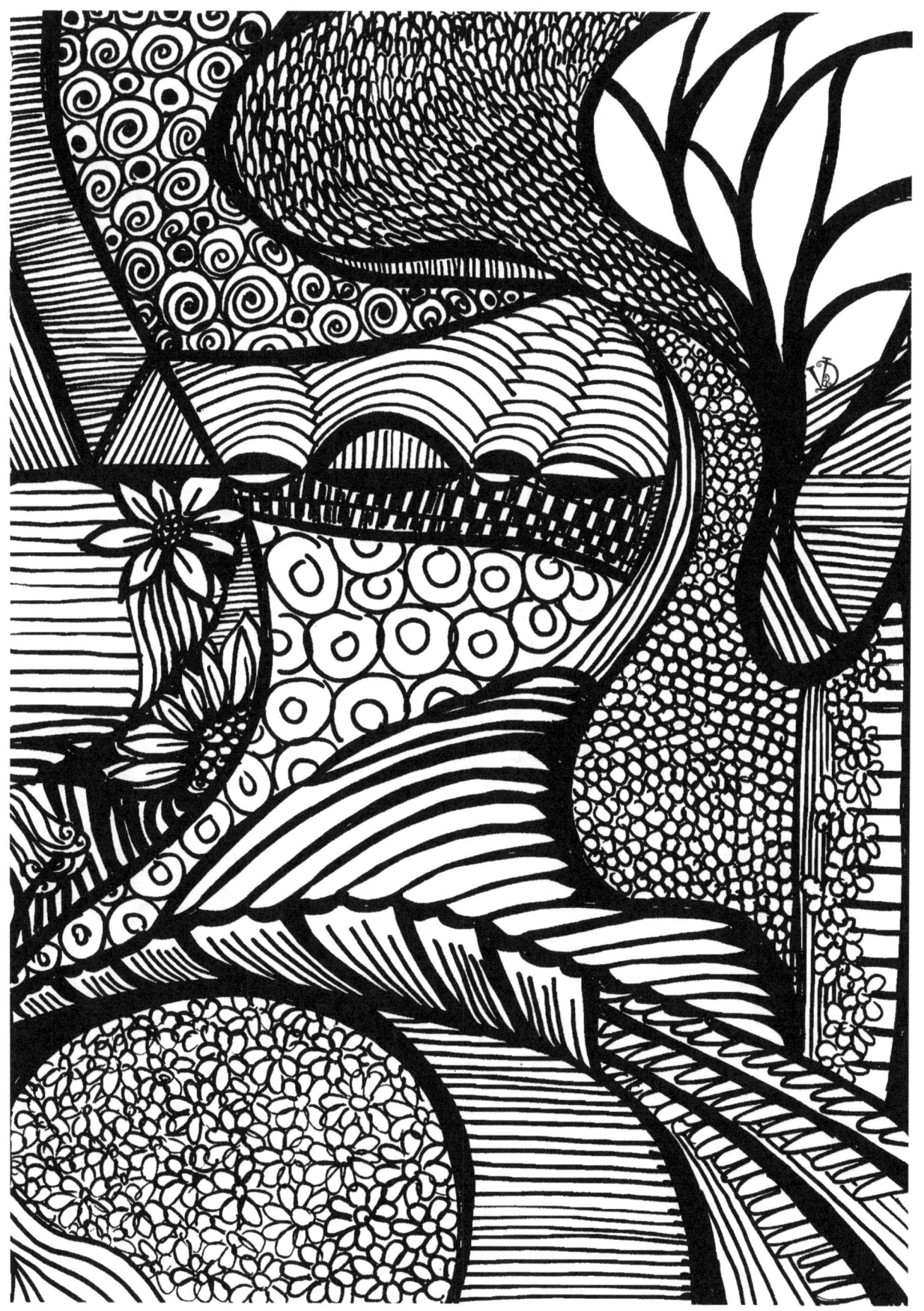

Abstract Expressions by Valerie Dowdy

Abstract Expressions by Valerie Dowdy

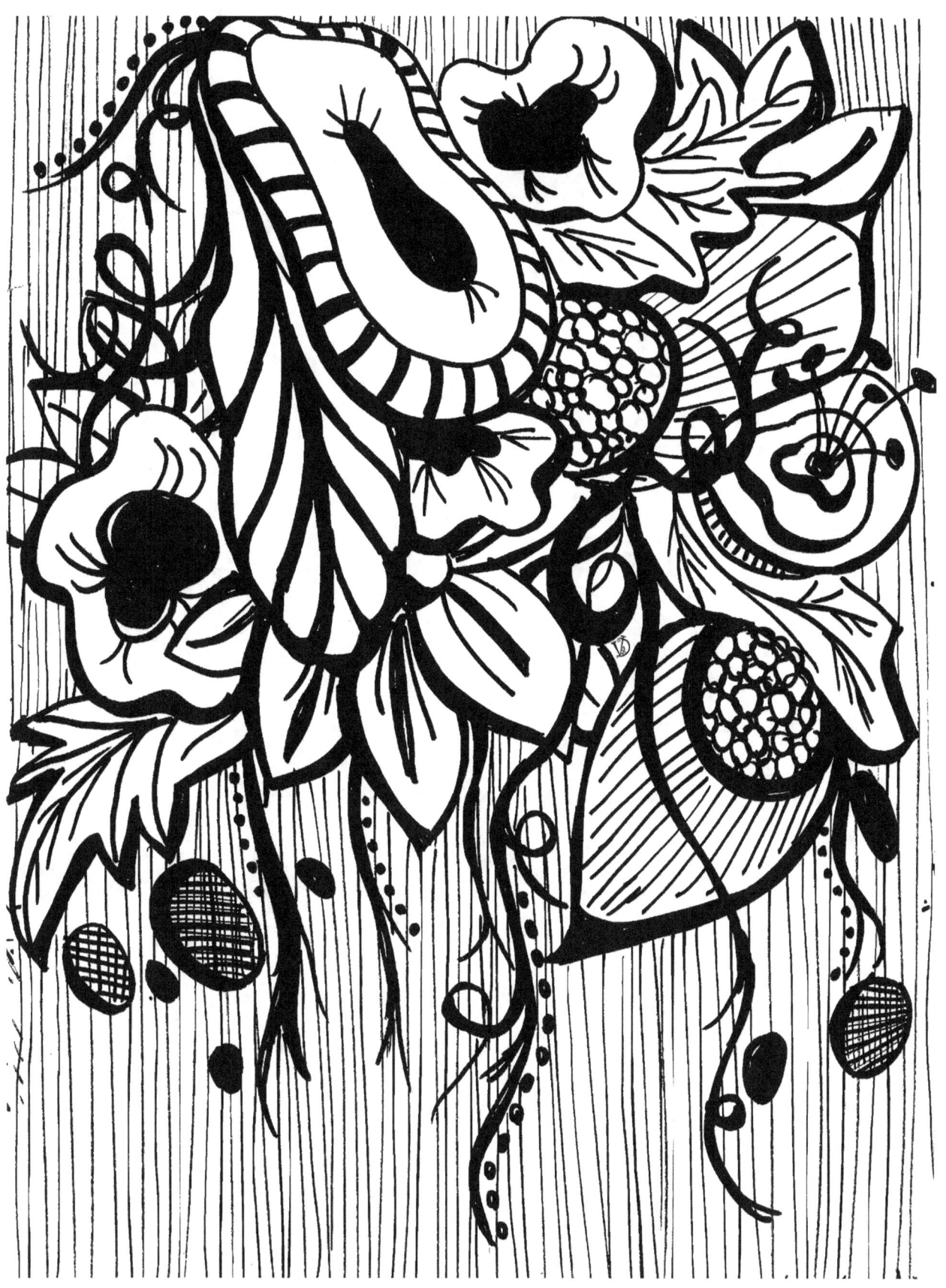

Abstract Expressions by Valerie Dowdy

Abstract Expressions by Valerie Dowdy

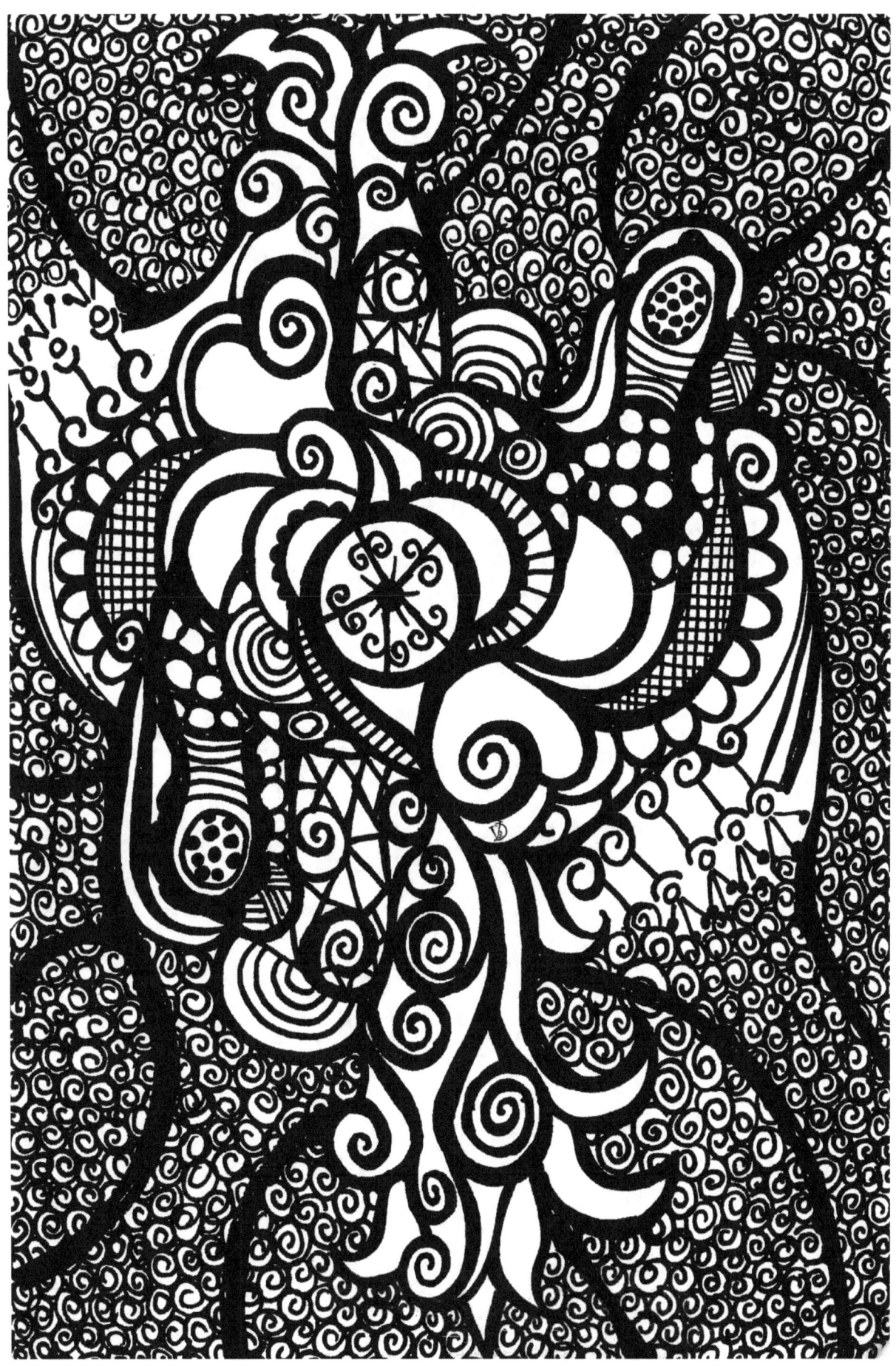

Abstract Expressions by Valerie Dowdy

Abstract Expressions by Valerie Dowdy

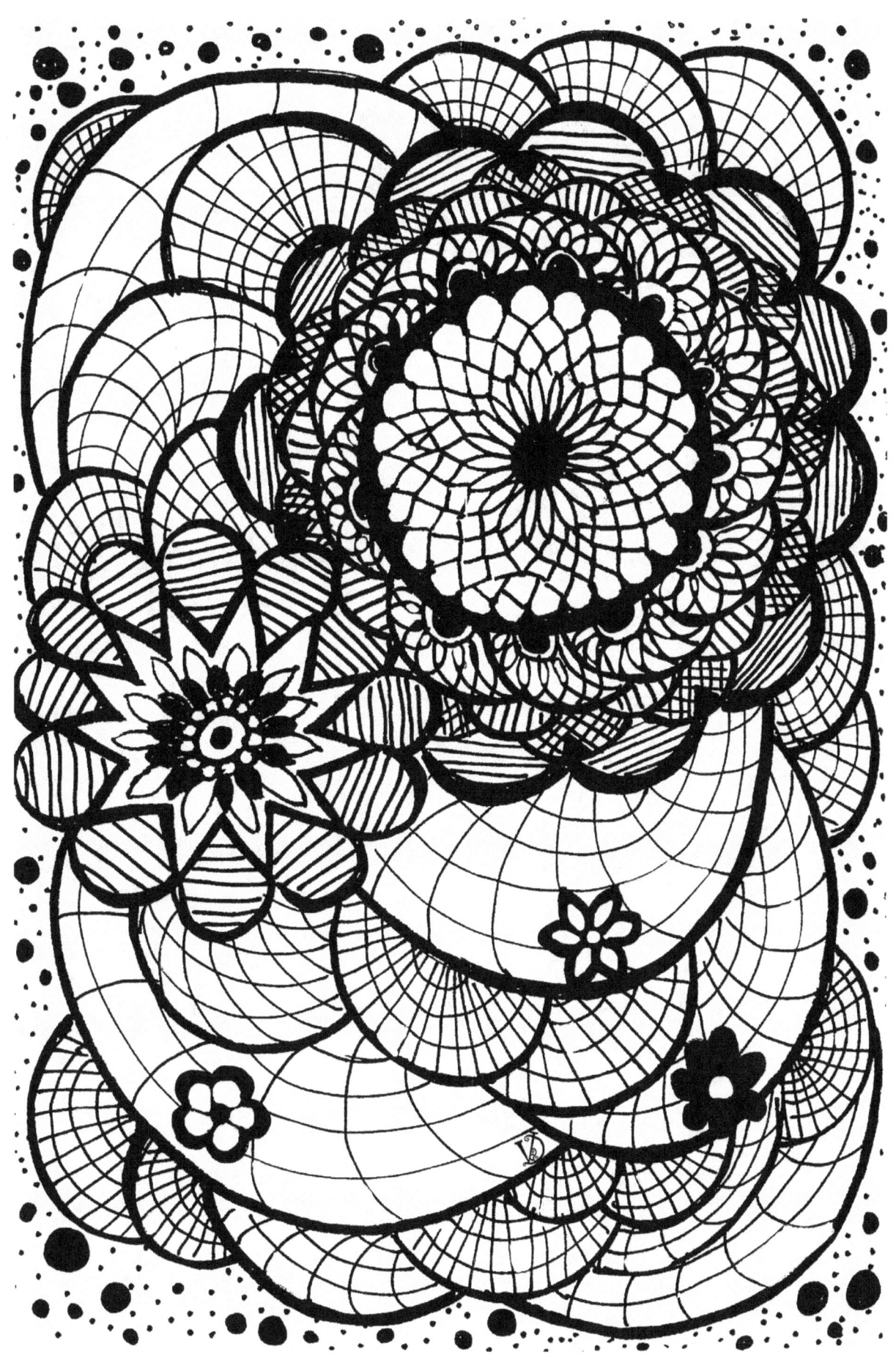

Abstract Expressions by Valerie Dowdy

Abstract Expressions by Valerie Dowdy

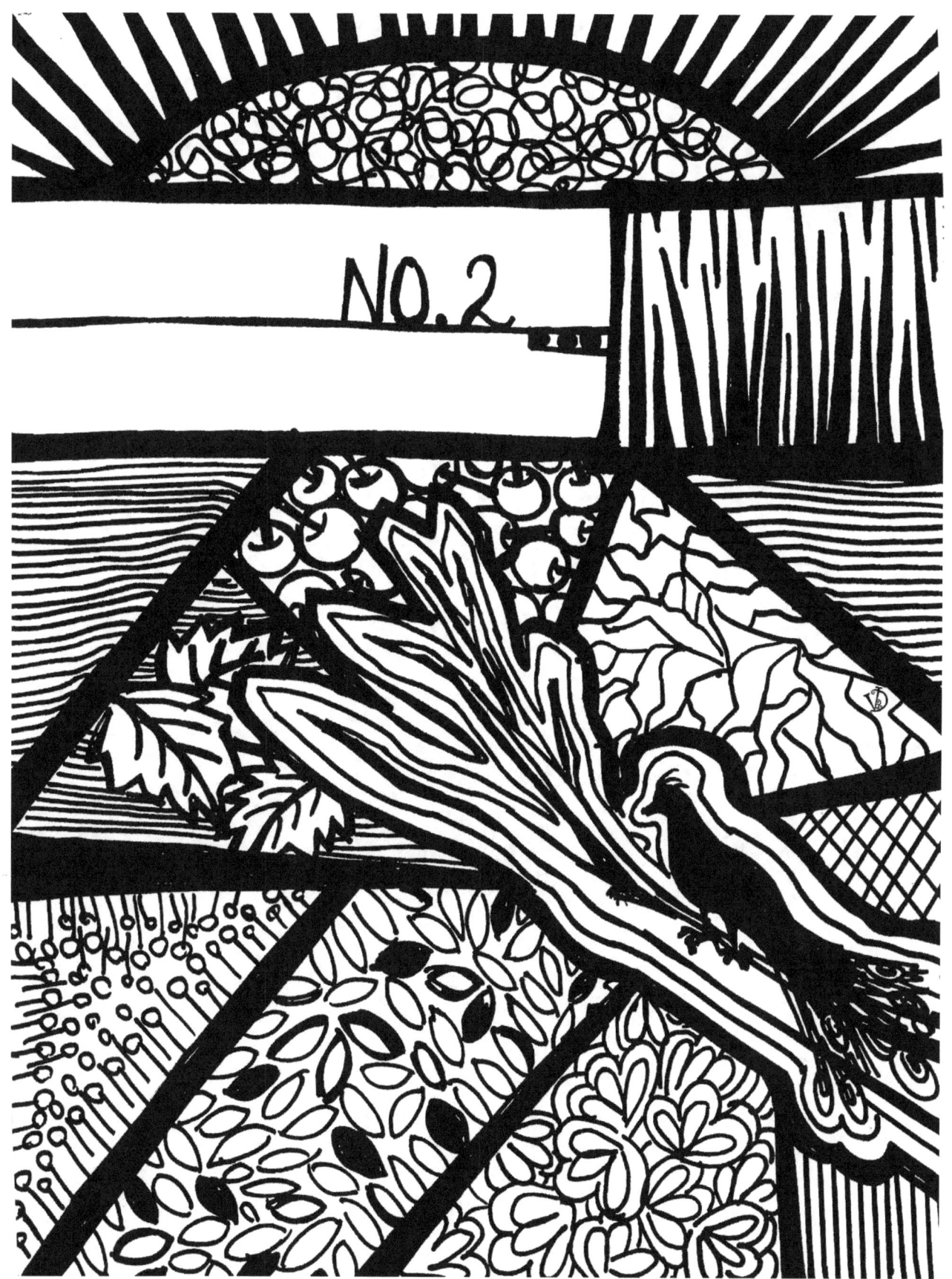

NO.2

Abstract Expressions by Valerie Dowdy

Abstract Expressions by Valerie Dowdy

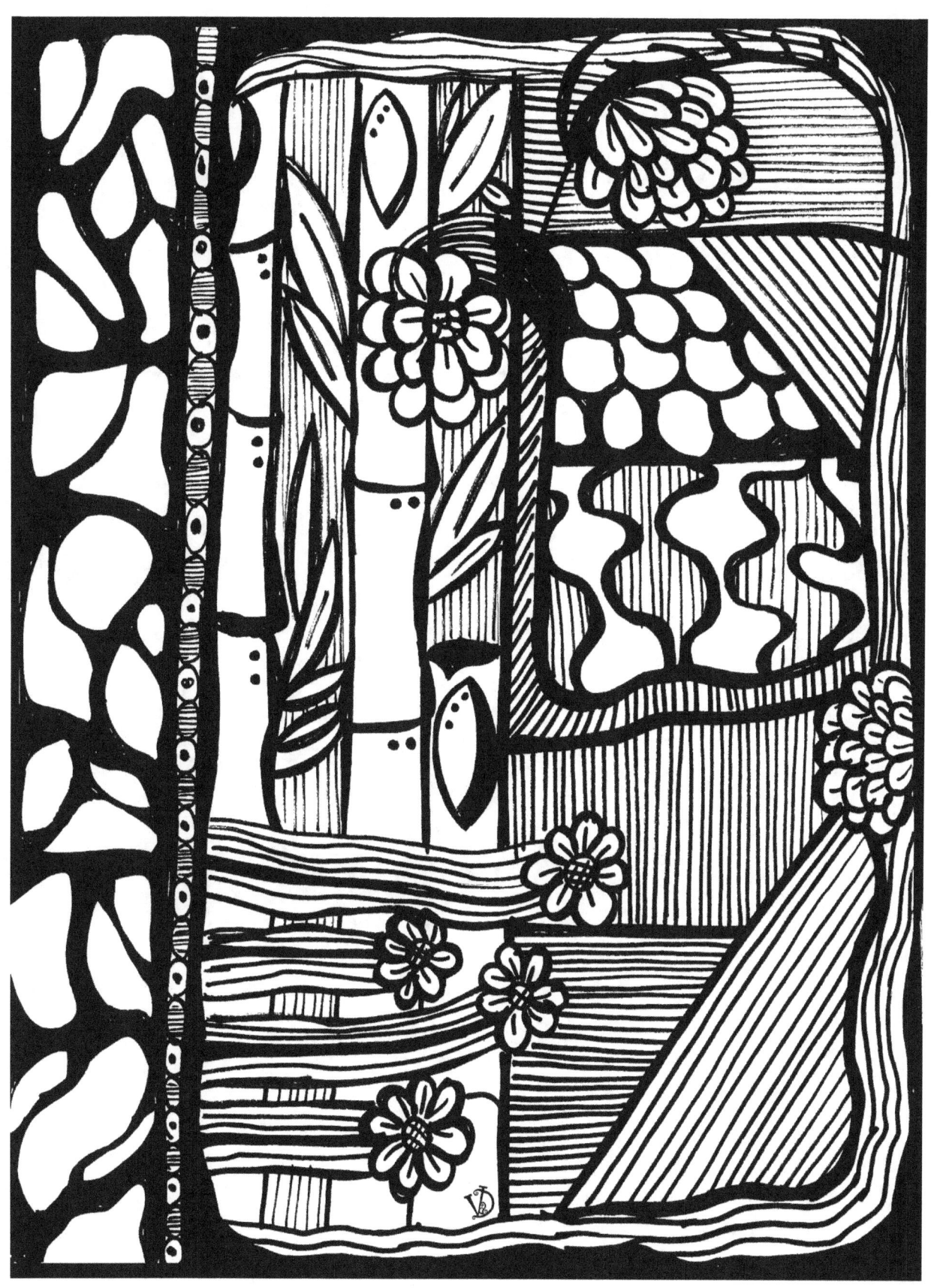

Abstract Expressions by Valerie Dowdy

Abstract Expressions by Valerie Dowdy

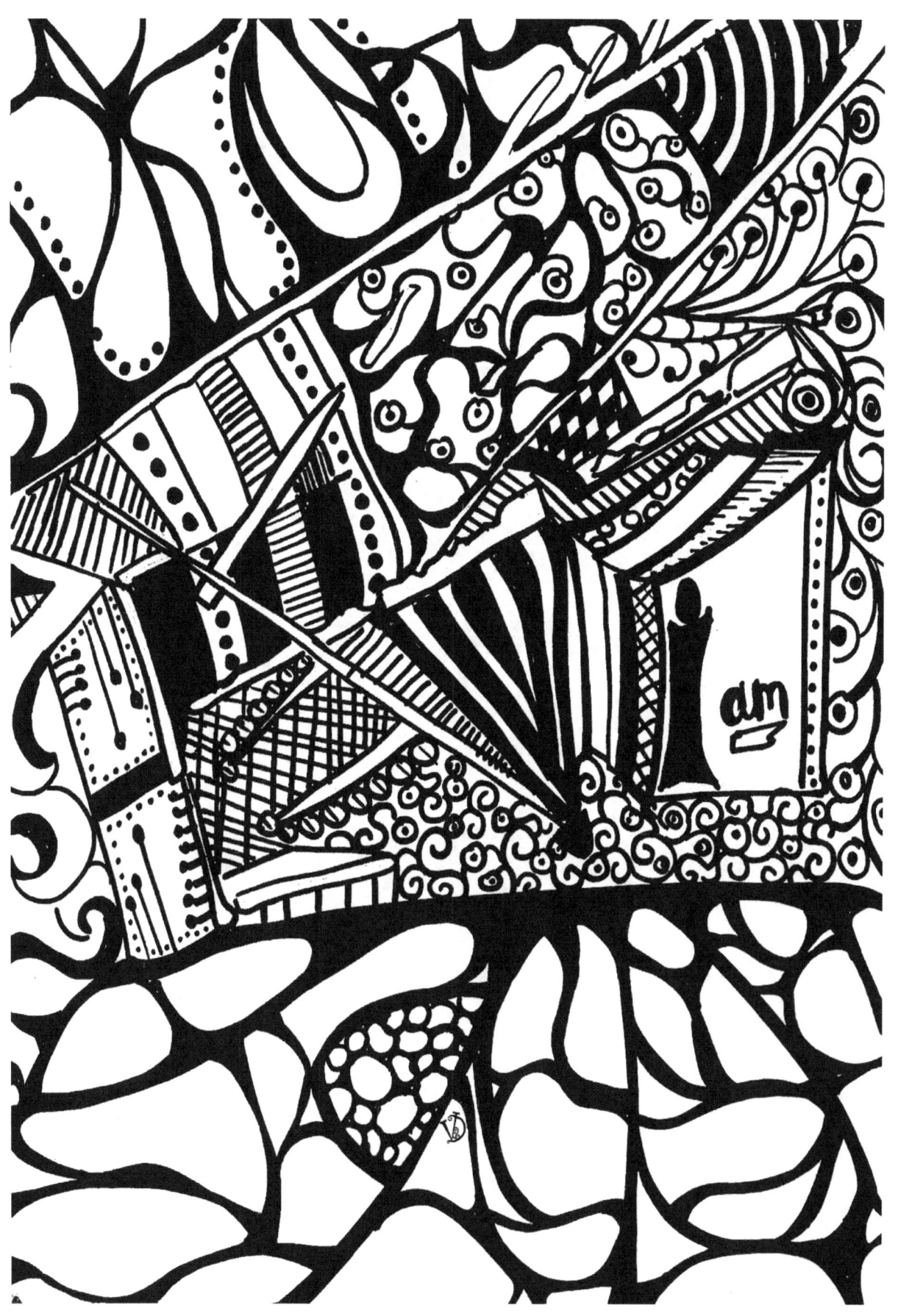

Abstract Expressions by Valerie Dowdy

Abstract Expressions by Valerie Dowdy

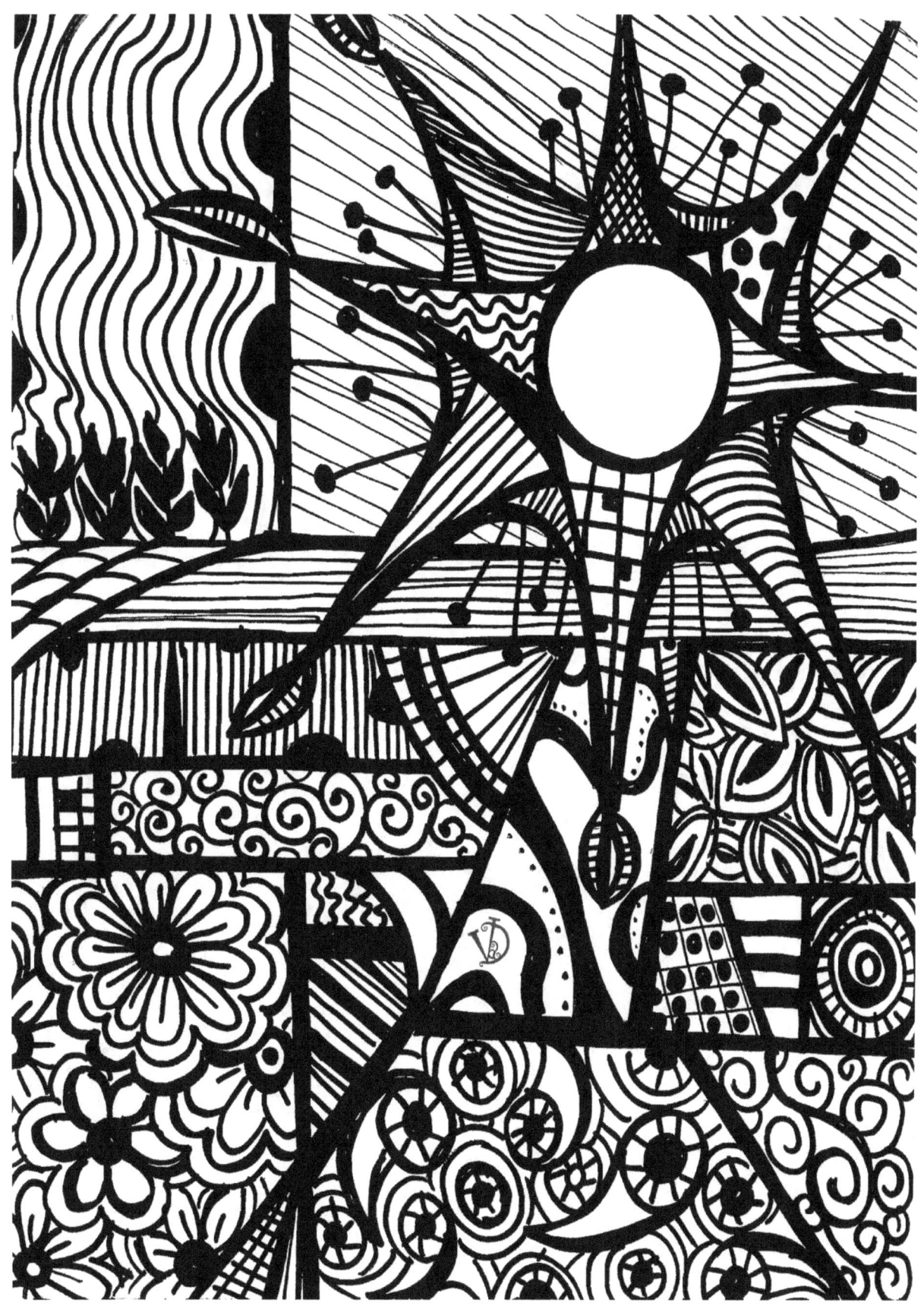

Abstract Expressions by Valerie Dowdy

Abstract Expressions by Valerie Dowdy

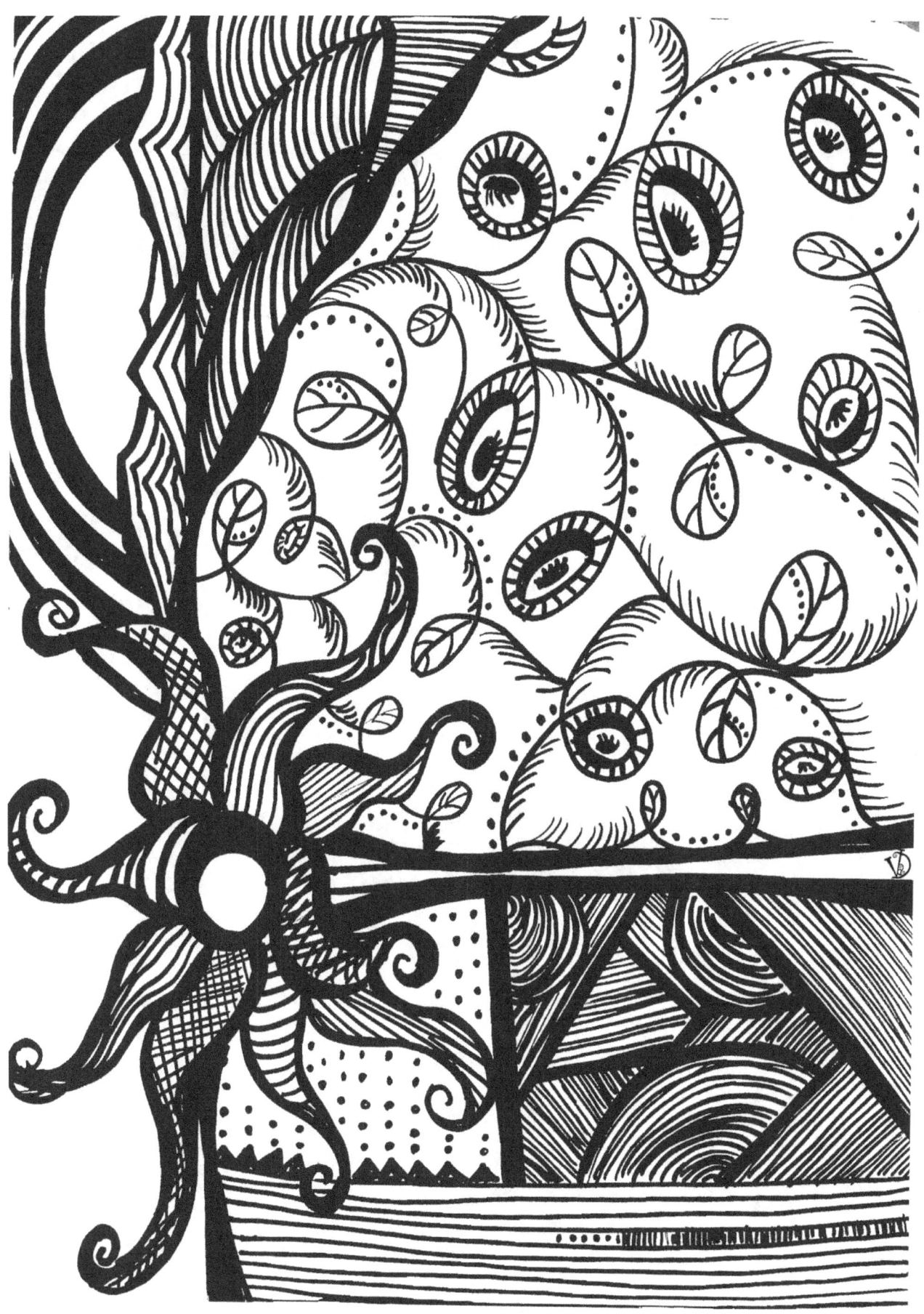

Abstract Expressions by Valerie Dowdy

Abstract Expressions by Valerie Dowdy

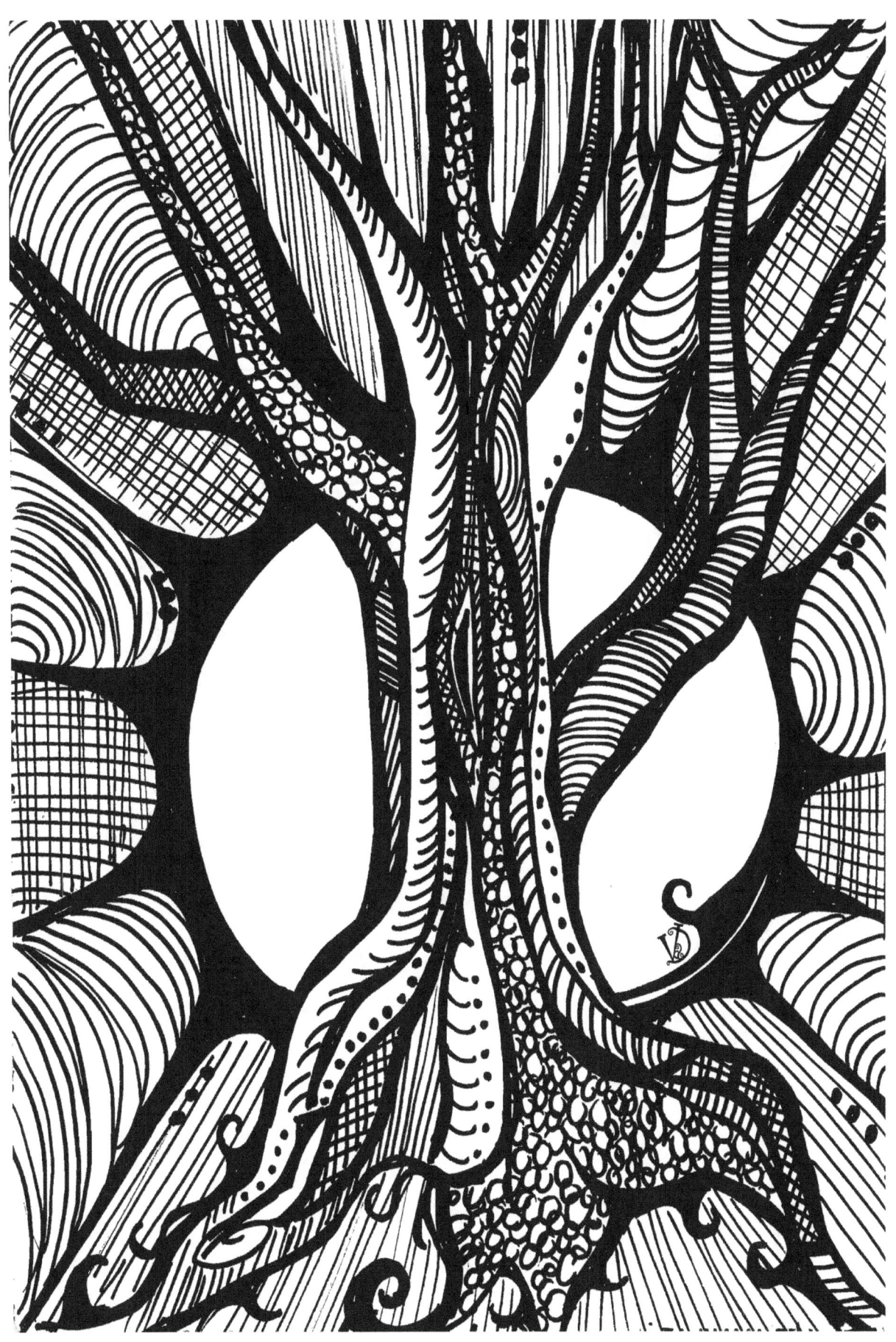

Abstract Expressions by Valerie Dowdy

Abstract Expressions by Valerie Dowdy

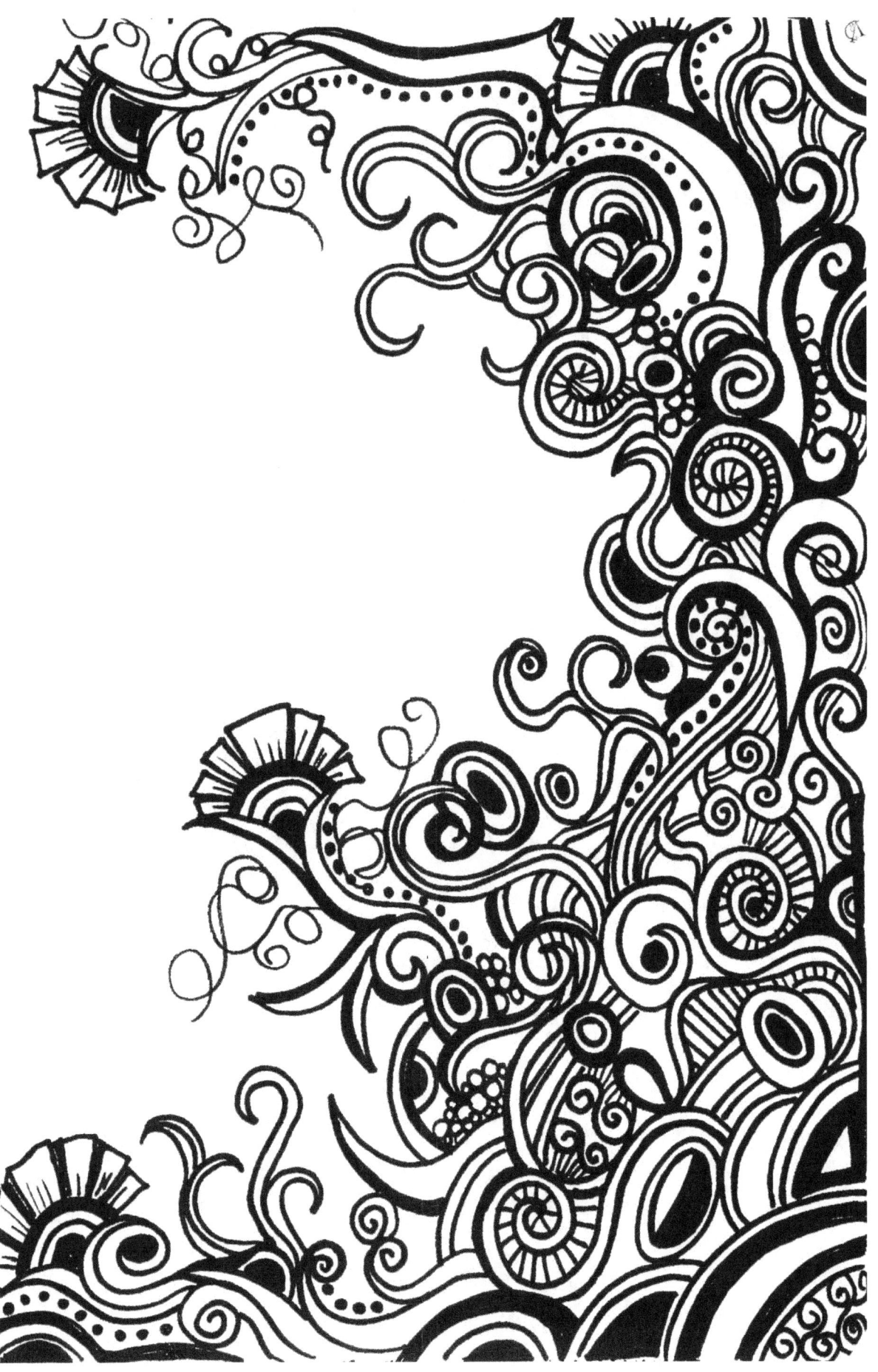

Abstract Expressions by Valerie Dowdy

Abstract Expressions by Valerie Dowdy

ABOUT THE AUTHOR

Valerie Dowdy is a visual artist living in Southwest Virginia, where she is developing a new body of work
that incorporates the intricate details taken from her art journal drawings and fusing them with a
surrealistic style of painting. It is also from these diaries that "Abstract Expressions" is produced.
Literally tearing pages from her journals, Valerie composed this coloring book in hopes
of helping others focus, relax and (re)connect with their own inner creativity.

Abstract Expressions by Valerie Dowdy